THE STIGLITZ REPORT

THE STIGLITZ REPORT

Reforming the International Monetary and Financial Systems in the Wake of the Global Crisis

Joseph E. Stiglitz

and Members of a

UN Commission of Financial Experts

With a foreword by Miguel d'Escoto Brockmann,

UN General Assembly President

THE NEW PRESS

NEW YORK
LONDON

© 2010 by The New Press
Preface © 2010 by Joseph E. Stiglitz
All rights reserved.
No part of this book may be reproduced, in any form, without
written permission from the publisher.

Requests for permission to reproduce selections from this book should be mailed to:
Permissions Department, The New Press, 38 Greene Street, New York, NY 10013.

Published in the United States by The New Press, New York, 2010
Distributed by Perseus Distribution

ISBN 978-1-59558-520-2 (pb)
CIP data available

The New Press was established in 1990 as a not-for-profit alternative to the large,
commercial publishing houses currently dominating the book publishing industry.
The New Press operates in the public interest rather than for private gain, and is
committed to publishing, in innovative ways, works of educational, cultural, and
community value that are often deemed insufficiently profitable.

www.thenewpress.com

Composition by Westchester Book Group

Printed in the United States of America

2   4   6   8   10   9   7   5   3   1

CONTENTS

LIST OF COMMISSION MEMBERS

Commission Members

Mr. Joseph E. Stiglitz (USA), chair
Mr. Andrei Bougrov (Russia)
Mr. Yousef Boutros-Ghali (Egypt)
Mr. Jean-Paul Fitoussi (France)
Mr. Charles A. Goodhart (UK)
Mr. Robert Johnson (USA)
Mr. Jomo Kwame Sundaram (UN)
Mr. Benno Ndulo (Tanzania)
Mr. José Antonio Ocampo (Colombia)
Mr. Pedro Páez (Ecuador)
Mr. Yaga Venugopal Reddy (India)
Mr. Avinash Persaud (Barbados)
Mr. Rubens Ricupero (Brazil)
Mr. Eisuke Sakakibara (Japan)
Mr. Chukwuma Soludo (Nigeria)
Ms. Heidemarie Wieczorek-Zeul (Germany)
Mr. Yu Yongding (China)
Ms. Zeti Akhtar Aziz (Malaysia)

Rapporteur

Mr. Jan Kregel (USA)

Special Representatives of the President of the General Assembly

Mr. François Houtart (Belgium)
Mr. Ali Boukrami (Algeria)

PREFACE

It was clear from the beginning that the U.S. crisis that began in 2007 would quickly become global. Even the early tremors in August of 2007 were felt most strongly thousands of miles away, in Indonesia. It was equally clear that there was a need for a global response but that the international economic and financial institutions were not fully up to the task. Indeed, some of these institutions had pushed the very policies of deregulation and financial and capital market liberalization that led to the crisis and its rapid spread around the world. The crisis exposed deep flaws in notions of market fundamentalism, the theory that unfettered markets would lead to efficient and stable outcomes. So too the idea that markets could be self-regulating was shown to be the oxymoron that it was. Yet, in at least some of the international economic institutions, these ideas had had pride of place.

This was, of course, not the first crisis facing the global economy. Just over ten years ago, there had been a major crisis in East Asia, which quickly morphed into a global financial crisis. In the aftermath of that crisis, there was much discussion of a new international financial architecture; but little was done—too little evidently. A new institution was created, the Financial Stability Forum, to ensure that another such crisis would not occur. But it too was guided by some of the same flawed economic models and philosophies, and not surprisingly it failed to prevent a crisis far worse than that which afflicted the world at the end of the last century.

Once again, it became evident that economic globalization had outpaced political globalization: the world had become more interdependent, and what happened in one country could have profound effects on others. Globalization meant that there was an increasing need for global collective action, for the countries of the world to act together, collectively and cooperatively. There was a need to make sure that one country didn't take actions that adversely affected others. The world should have done this *before the crisis.*

A CALL FOR GLOBAL ACTION

But now that the crisis had occurred, there was a need for concerted action to ensure a quick recovery. As we emphasize in Chapter 2, efforts by one country to stimulate its economy would benefit others, as that country imported more. There were large positive externalities in providing a strong stimulus; but there were strong incentives for each country to be a free-rider on the efforts of others. Even worse was the risk of the kind of beggar-thy-neighbor policies that had marked the Great Depression, as each country tried to stimulate its own economy at the expense of others. The only way around this problem was for all the countries of the world to cooperate to provide a large global stimulus.

There was also need for the world to come to the help of the developing countries. Help was motivated not only by humanitarian concerns but also by self-interest—it would be hard to have a sustained global recovery if one part of the world remained in recession. Moreover, such an unbalanced recovery, if it occurred, could exacerbate global imbalances, which had threatened global stability in the years before the crisis.

But there was also a sense of moral culpability: the developing countries were innocent victims of America's mismanagement of its economy.

There was a second sense in which the United States and other advanced industrial countries had a moral culpability: they had foisted on unwary developing countries liberalization policies *without appropriate safeguards.* These policies had exposed the developing countries to enormous risk; but the developing countries still did not have the resources to deal with the consequences. The developed countries were spending hundreds of billions of dollars to help their citizens cope and to help stabilize their economies. The developing countries could not follow suit.

The blame should not rest just with the governments of the developed countries and the international financial institutions. More broadly, financial markets had been influential in encouraging the developing countries' adoption of the Washington Consensus policies, which had served the developing countries so poorly, even as they served the banks so well. Before the last crisis, the banks of the advanced industrial countries had made money as funds rushed into East Asia. Their banks had been absolved of bearing the cost of their mistakes, as taxpayers in these countries in the end funded the bailouts—repaying, with interest, the IMF and others who had come to the rescue of the banks. And then they had made money once again in the rescue, in the fire sales of the East Asian companies that the IMF had demanded as the price for its assistance.

In this crisis, the banks would, once again, be bailed out, this time by American and European taxpayers.

Finally, there was a need for the international community to adopt new regulatory standards if we were not to have a repeat of the current crisis a few years down the line. The old standards had clearly failed. This crisis was simply the worst in a string of crises that had plagued the world since the era of deregulation had begun—more than one hundred crises in thirty years, in marked contrast to the absence of crises in the previous half century, when the world seemed to have learned the lessons of the Great Depression and adopted and enforced strong regulations. Unless something was done, almost surely, there would be more crises in the not-too-distant future.

TAKING THE LEAD: WEAKNESSES IN GLOBAL GOVERNANCE

The need for international action across a broad front was clear. But who could or would take the lead? The United States couldn't—its flawed macro-economics, based on a set of flawed ideas, had led to the global mess; besides, President Bush was committed to undermining multilateralism. This was a global crisis, so a small club—the G-7 or G-8—wasn't up to the task either. Besides, it was clear that money would be needed, and the large reserves were held in Asia and the Middle East, in countries that were not members of the club.

The IMF had come to the rescue of the global financial system before. But it too was not well suited for this occasion. After all, it certainly had neither seen the crisis coming nor fulfilled its responsibilities in preventing the crisis, and, as I noted earlier, it was one of those that had pushed on developing countries the very policies for which it bore much of the blame. Potential borrowers in the developing countries were loath to turn to the IMF, given how it had treated those that sought help in the past. It lacked adequate funding, and those with money in the Middle East and Asia were skeptical of the institution: after all, the IMF was dominated by the United States and the other advanced industrial countries (the United States still was the only country with a veto, and Europe always appointed its head) that were responsible for the crisis.

Two institutions stepped into this void. The G-20 finance ministers had been meeting regularly since a decade earlier at the time of the East Asia crisis. Now, at the initiative of European leaders, the G-20 members were being elevated to the level of leaders. But there are 192 countries in the world—and that meant the voices of some 172 wouldn't be heard. Moreover, while the G-20 represented some 75% of the world's GDP, it lacked representativeness and political legitimacy. While it was understandable why some countries were in the "club," it wasn't clear why others were—or why others were not. The developing countries and the smaller countries were especially aggrieved. Only one country in sub-Saharan Africa was at the table—South Africa—and it could hardly speak for the other African countries that were so different.

THE ESTABLISHMENT OF THE COMMISSION

The United Nations was the one international organization with the legitimacy to bring all the countries of the world together. The President of the General Assembly recognized the importance of the UN taking action. He called for a summit or a high-level meeting on the crisis, one that would especially focus on the impacts of the crisis on the developing countries, whose concerns, he worried, might otherwise be given short shrift. He approached me to chair a Commission of Experts, which would both yield an independent report on the crisis and what should be done, as well as help set the agenda for the summit.

An expert panel has some distinct advantages. It can be forthright in its analysis of the causes; it doesn't have to be quite as diplomatic in assigning blame. In solutions, it can broach new ideas—ideas that might not be enthusiastically endorsed by all countries, because they might hamper special and influential interests. These ideas might not be translated into policies immediately, but they could help set the agenda for the future.

From the beginning, it was clear that the processes of our Commission and the G-20 could be complementary. We did not see them as rival, but as mutually supportive. In the end, decisions have to be made through political processes; but an expert panel could help shape those processes.

The Commission was established by the President of the General Assembly in October 2008.

THE MEMBERS OF THE COMMISSION

In putting together the expert panel, we sought to have a diversity of perspectives and viewpoints. This would make getting consensus more difficult, but it would mean that any consensus would be more meaningful. We were pleased that almost everyone we approached agreed to serve on the Commission—though we knew that all had extraordinarily busy schedules; they shared our conviction of the potential importance of such a Commission.

We looked for people who had been crisis veterans—like Governor Zeti, who had played a central role in Malaysia's successful navigation of the East Asia crisis a decade earlier. Malaysia had emerged from the crisis more quickly, with less of an overhang of debt, than had the other East Asian countries. But even before the crisis, Malaysia had shown great wisdom in managing the risks of global financial markets, by insisting that not only its banks but also the firms to which its banks lent did not have excessive exposure to foreign exchange risk. Eisuke Sakakibara as Japan's Vice Minister of Finance for International Affairs during the East Asian crisis had deservedly earned a reputation for thoughtful and innovative approaches, such as the creation of an Asian Monetary Fund.

We looked for those who had done a better job in managing their country's monetary policy in the run up to the crisis by imposing regulations that curtailed excessive risk-taking yet allowed robust growth—people like Governor Zeti and Governor Reddy, who was just stepping down as head of the Reserve Bank of India. We wanted people with a diverse set of backgrounds, including those who had lived multiple lives, like Charles Goodhart, then teaching at the London School of Economics, but who had served on the UK's Monetary Policy Committee, and Jose Antonio Ocampo, a distinguished economic historian, then teaching at Columbia, who had served as Under-Secretary-General of the UN for Economic and Social Affairs under Kofi Annan, had been head of the UN Economic Commission for Latin America, and had served at various times as Colombia's minister of planning, finance, and agriculture. He had helped introduce that country's system of moderating surges of capital flows—short-term capital flows had repeatedly been a source of instability in developing countries, and were playing a critical role in the rapid spread of the crisis around the world. Andrei Bougrov, a prominent Russian businessman, had been that country's executive director at the World Bank during Russia's ruble crisis a decade earlier. Rob Johnson had served as chief economist of the Senate Banking Committee in the early 1980s, as attempts to deregulate were mounting, and had gone on to have a highly successful career in financial markets (including a stint working with George Soros's hedge fund).

We especially wanted expertise in development. Our worry was that the developing countries would be among the hardest hit by the downturn—and we were correct. Heidemarie Wieczorek-Zeul had fought tirelessly as Germany's Minister of Cooperation and Development to provide assistance to the poorest countries, and it was important that any emergency assistance be integrated with longer term development assistance. Two of Africa's most distinguished economists cum central bankers, Charles Soludo from Nigeria, and Ben Ndulo from Tanzania, agreed to serve on the panel. We sought representation from the smaller countries—Avi Persaud from Barbados also brought an unparalleled expertise in financial markets from his then position as Chairman of Intelligence Capital in London, and

Pedro Paez from Ecuador also brought a unique experience in deal-ing with his country's debt problem.

The impacts of the crisis would be felt especially through an unprecedented drop off in trade, and it was thus important to have expertise on the relationship between trade and finance. Rubens Ri-cupero, formerly head of UNCTAD, the UN Commission on Trade and Development, and former minister of finance of Brazil, brought this expertise, as did Jan Kregel, formerly at UNCTAD but then serv-ing as Senior Scholar for the Levy Economics Institute at Bard Col-lege, who served as rapporteur.

The crisis would require a concerted international response, which was why it was important to have expertise on the international insti-tutions. Many members of the Commission had served in one capac-ity or another at various such institutions (Kregel, Ricupero, Bougrov, Stiglitz, Ocampo). All of the central bank governors served as "gover-nors" of the IMF and many had participated in meetings of the BIS, the Bank of International Settlement, in Basel, where the central banks gather to discuss their common problems and approaches. In addition, K. S. Jomo, a distinguished Malaysian academic, was serv-ing as assistant secretary of the UN Department of Economic and Social Affairs and head of research for the G-24, a grouping of 24 de-veloping countries seeking to advance their views about international economic policy within the international economic institutions.

It was important to have a representative of the world's largest emerg-ing market, China, and we were fortunate in getting the active participa-tion of Yu Yongding from the Chinese Academy of Social Sciences, a distinguished academic whose analyses of global imbalances and the global reserve system had already drawn international attention. By the same token, it was clear that the global imbalances were related to macro-economic imbalances, and that macro-economic management would be a critical issue going forward. Jean-Paul Fitoussi, head of the French Economic Observatory (OFCE) and one of the world's leading macro-economists, agreed to serve on the Commission.

Ali Boukrami from Algeria and Yousef Boutros-Gali from Egypt brought a Middle Eastern perspective to the table. And Francois Houtart, from Belgium, ensured that the Commission saw the current global financial crisis within the broader perspective of the other crises afflicting the developing countries—including the food, energy, and climatic crises.

Members of the Commission also brought different academic perspectives to bear. While members were well-versed in neoclassical doctrines—notions that markets were efficient and self-correcting—they also understood the limitations of those doctrines and their underpinning assumptions. Goodhart had long explored "availability doctrines" in monetary policy—the notion that monetary policy exerts its influence not just through interest rates but also through access to finance. Kregel had been a leader in developing ideas associated with credit bubbles pioneered by Hyman Minsky. Stiglitz had helped develop neo-Keynesian economics, particularly the branch associated with understanding the consequences of debt and credit markets—especially important in this crisis associated with excess leverage.

While several members of the panel had official positions, all served in their individual capacities. They brought their expertise and their commitment to the work of the Commission without being encumbered by the constraints that would inevitably follow from their having to reflect their "official" positions. At the same time, the close connections between many of the members of the Commission and "officialdom" facilitated the work of the Commission being given serious consideration.

THE DELIBERATION PROCESS

The first meeting of the Commission was held in early January 2009. At this meeting, the work program of the Commission was agreed upon. Four working groups were established, reflected in the four main chapters of the report. It was clear that this was not just a financial crisis but also an economic crisis. The financial sector had misallocated capital, with a massive loss in societal wealth. But the real losses in output would come after America's real estate bubble broke, as actual output fell short of potential output in countries around the world. Managing the aftermath of the breaking of the bubble would be one of the important challenges going forward; hence, the first working group focused on macro-economics and was headed by Fitoussi. Lack of regulation was central to the creation of the crisis and its rapid spread; hence, the second working group was chaired by Persaud. International institutions would have to play an important role in the resolution of the crisis, but for them to be fully effective there had to be significant reforms; understanding what was needed was the focus of the third working group, for which Jomo served as chair. Finally, members of the Commission thought it important to think "out of the box," to initiate discussions of some more fundamental reforms—reforms that might not be accomplished immediately, but were necessary for long-run sustainable growth. The fourth working group focused on these medium to longer term measures and was headed by Ocampo.

Following the January meeting in New York, the working groups and the Commission as a whole met in Kuala Lumpur (February), New York (February), Berlin (March), Geneva (March), The Hague (May), and in New York, at the time of the report on our preliminary findings (in March), and at the time of the summit meeting (June).

The discussions were lively and intense, but good spirited: in the end, a remarkable consensus was reached on almost all of the issues. In a few cases, there was agreement about a set of principles and objectives with some differences about the best way to achieve the objectives. It was our hope that our report would serve as the beginning of discussions on some of these vital areas, and so we thought it important to lay out the alternatives, and the arguments for each.

HOW GREATER REPRESENTATIVENESS MAKES A DIFFERENCE

Anyone reading our report will, I think, grasp the advantages of an expert panel. I hope the reader will agree that the analytic foundations are clearer and more forceful than those that emerge from the typical governmental report. Popular discussions have focused on the role of excess liquidity and low interest rates; but our discussions push the analysis of why the Fed pursued such policies—a perhaps politically delicate issue that the Bush administration would have been hesitant about the G-20 broaching. There has been widespread concern about global imbalances, but explaining the global imbalances also touches on politically sensitive issues—including the way the last global financial crisis was managed by the IMF and the U.S. Treasury.

Similarly, we could broach solutions that one or the other major powers might find inconvenient, such as the reform of the global reserve system. We could raise questions about the adequacy of certain difficult-to-reach political compromises.

There is another question for which the answer is not so obvious: did our efforts at greater representativeness (than say the G-20) make a difference? And if so, how? I believe it did, and the fact that it did has important lessons for global governance going forward.

Four issues serve to illustrate. First, the G-20 turned to the IMF as the international institution to provide assistance to developing countries. This was a natural choice, since the IMF had played a central role in bailouts and rescues in earlier decades. But that constituted part of the problem: the way the IMF had performed that role had cost it support in many developing countries—countries whose voice was not adequately heard at the G-20 meetings. Some poor countries made it clear that they would seek help from individual countries with reserves and would turn to the IMF only as a last resort. Moreover, the IMF's credibility had been badly hurt by its long-standing support for the deregulation and liberalization policies that were central to creating the crisis and its rapid spread. Still further problems were created because many of the countries with large reserves in Asia and the Middle East were hesitant to turn over their money to the IMF: not only did they have inadequate voice and representation but also many of the policies that the IMF had pursued were contrary to those that these governments believed in. A final problem was presented by the fact that the IMF typically provides money through short-term loans. Many of the poor countries were just emerging from under an overhang of debt; they did not want to find themselves in the same situation again. Moreover, while the worst of the crisis would pass, the global economy might not return to robust growth quickly.

Many developing countries were reluctant to turn to the IMF for another reason: in the past crises, its assistance had been accompanied by procyclical conditionality—reductions in expenditures and tightening of interest rates, just the opposite of the Keynesian policies pursued by the advanced industrial countries in this crisis.

Relying on the IMF risked undermining an effective multilateral response. Reforms in the IMF (some of which were accelerated through the efforts of the G-20) were very helpful. The IMF supported countercyclical policies; in some cases, it even supported the imposition of capital controls. It allowed countries to maintain much larger deficits than in the past. Its managing director emphasized the risks of a too-early withdrawal of stimulus and emphasized that the strength of recovery should be judged not just on what happened to GDP but also on the reduction of unemployment to more normal levels. At the same time, it was clear that some of the reforms, such as in governance, did not go far enough, were not occurring fast enough (see Chapter 4), and would not in the short run fully restore confidence in that institution. Moreover, of the large amounts given to the IMF, only a fraction would go to the developing countries. Our Commission drew attention to these limitations, called for a more diverse set of mechanisms for disbursement of assistance, with more of the assistance in the form of grants, and suggested the creation of a new facility. Had our suggestions been followed, the magnitude of the downturn in some developing countries might have been smaller.

A second example is provided by the discussion of offshore banking centers, which have been the focus of tax avoidance and evasion. While these centers had little to do with the crisis, they were a source of long-standing concern for the global financial system, and it was perhaps natural to center discussion around actions by countries that were not at the table to defend themselves. It was clear to the Commission that (a) the actions proposed by the G-20 did not go far enough; (b) delegating responsibility for ascertaining which countries were "noncooperative" to the OECD, an organization of the advanced industrial countries was inappropriate; (c) there were serious problems of lack of transparency in some of the G-20 countries; and (d) tax evasion/ avoidance is not the only problem. There are problems of money laundering associated with drugs; secret bank accounts hide money stolen by corrupt dictators—but even when such funds are discovered, some of the G-20 countries refuse to repatriate it. These criticisms were given further support by the Tax Justice Network, which criticized both the United States and the UK for bank secrecy.*

In this case, our views made it not only into the Outcome document of the June UN Summit but also into the Pittsburgh meeting of the G-20, held in September.

The third example concerns the discussion of regulation. Though everyone acknowledged the need for regulatory reform, there was a major split between Europe and the United States. France and the UK were adamant about the need for changing the financial executive bonus system; the United States, at the time, was reluctant to touch the issue—given the opposition of America's powerful financial lobby. When there are such divisions within the G-20, it is nearly impossible for them to say anything strong. For an expert group, this was an easy issue: the one thing economists agree on is that incentives matter, and the typical financial executive's incentive scheme encourages short-sighted behavior and excessive risk-taking. What had happened was predictable and predicted.

Because incentives matter, the Commission expressed strong concerns about the too-big-to-fail banks: when these gamble and win, they walk away with the profits; when they lose, taxpayers pick up the tab. The distortions in incentives are obvious. But given the political influence of the big banks, it is perhaps not surprising that the G-20, at least in its initial meetings, made no mention of the issue.

The final example was the suggestion of the Commission for reforms of the global reserve system. Here our concerns that the current arrangements contributed to an inadequacy of global aggregate demand—and might hamper a strong recovery—have now become widely accepted. Most of the reserves today are held by emerging markets (in Asia and the Middle East), and these markets worry about the loss in value of these reserves with the declining value of the dollar. For a long time it seemed anomalous to have the global financial system be

---

* In the Tax Justice Network's Financial Secrecy Index, the United States ranks first and the U.K. ranks fifth in legal and financial secrecy. See, "Financial Secrecy Index," Tax Justice Network, available at http://www.financialsecrecyindex.com.

so dependent on the currency of a single country; but with America's looming deficits and the ballooning of the Fed's balance sheet as the United States responded to the crisis, these concerns moved front and center. Yet the United States was reluctant to have the subject broached, even though many economists believed that the current system worked not only to the disadvantage of the developing countries but even to the disadvantage of the United States, as the large trade deficits—the flip side of the growing holdings of dollar reserves—weakened U.S. aggregate demand. But more apparent than this disadvantage was the immediate advantage of being able to borrow at low interest rates—an advantage that was particularly relevant with the largest deficits that somehow had to be financed. It was thus no surprise that while economists from both the developed and developing countries saw reforming the global reserve system as central to addressing the problems of global imbalances, the G-20 shied away from the issue.

IDEAS MATTER

One of the reasons for bringing to the table a more diverse set of countries and individuals is not just that their concerns differ, but that there may also be a greater diversity of ideas. And ideas matter. A particular set of ideas had led to deregulation and other policies (both in the private and public sectors) that contributed to the crisis and to its rapid spread. Another, quite different set of ideas led to the strong policies to combat the crisis. Almost no country said, let the markets take care of themselves; and even the free market fundamentalists within the market came running to the government for help.

To too large an extent before the crisis, a dominant orthodoxy prevailed—a set of ideas that proved wanting. If the world was to move into a robust recovery and prevent a recurrence, a broader set of ideas had to be given serious consideration. It is only through robust debate among people who see the world through different lenses that the validity of different perspectives can be assessed.

There is often a complex interplay between ideas, ideologies, and interests. The financial markets had an interest in arguing for deregulation; the free market ideology served them well. But if economics is to emerge as a social science, its postulates have to be tested. This crisis has called into question many widely held assumptions.

SIX MONTHS LATER AND THE AGENDA AHEAD

As this introduction goes to press, some six months later—and one year after the Commission began its work—the world seems relieved to have apparently pulled back from the financial brink so quickly. Much has been accomplished. The international community should, in many ways, be pleased with these successes.

The Monterrey Meeting on Finance for Development in 2003 had shown that the UN could and should play an important role in shaping the development agenda—as it had done three years earlier, in creating the Millennium Development Goals. Finance, and even more so, the overall economy, is too important to be left to Finance and Economy Ministers. The G-20 established the same proposition.

Still, as we look at the global economy in January 2010, there is reason for concern. In most countries, the financial sector has successfully beat back attempts at key regulatory and institutional reforms. The financial sector is more concentrated; the problems of moral hazard are worse. Global imbalances remain unabated.

It remains clear that the market economy faces enormous volatility. Financial markets did not manage the risks well before the crisis; developing countries had long been left bearing the burden of exchange rate and interest rate risks. If past crises are any guide to the future, there is the risk of severe "aftershocks" as some countries cannot bear the burden of debt accumulated during the crisis and as global interest rates rise in response to the increased demand for funds as a result of enormous government borrowing.

While the international community has recognized the need for better mechanisms for risk sharing and bearing—a subject discussed in Chapter 5 of this report—progress is slow. The IMF has made some proposals entailing increased reliance on that institution, which would reduce the need for the growing reserves (which, in turn, have contributed to weaknesses in global aggregate demand, as we noted earlier). The problem is that, so far, most developing countries do not have enough confidence in the IMF to abandon their self-reliance through reserves. Matters might change if there were a longer track record, or if its governance changed along the lines suggested in Chapter 4. But neither of these will occur quickly, presenting problems for the robust recovery of the global economy.

We face a world with huge unmet needs—adapting to climate change, reducing carbon emissions, and fighting poverty—but with underutilized resources. Unemployment in Europe and the United States is at or exceeds 10%. One in six Americans who would like a full-time job cannot get one. Yet the response from some quarters was to encourage China to consume more. The world should not be trying to imitate the profligate lifestyle of the United States—our planet cannot withstand it. The real challenge is to find better ways to recycle savings to where it is needed.

This brings me back to one of the themes of the Commission, one which several of the members continually emphasized: we should see this crisis not in isolation, but in conjunction with the series of crises that the world has faced in recent years—the food, climate change, and energy crises.

As fears of another depression fade, discussions have turned to "exit," cutting back on the massive government stimulus programs and the unusual monetary measures. Doing so may prove difficult, and dealing with the aftermath of the crisis may prove even more challenging: the high levels of indebtedness will impose large costs even on advanced industrial countries, and these countries were already facing serious budgetary difficulties in the coming years with the aging of the baby boomers. Cutbacks in social insurance may fray the fragile social contract, already tattered by the bank bailouts, and cutbacks in investments in infrastructure, education, and technology will slow growth.

The Commission was appointed to serve for a short period; its mandate expired with the end of the term of the President of the General Assembly. But the challenges facing the international community continue. The consequences of the failures of America's financial system for the United States and countries around the globe will be felt for years to come. The world after the crisis will be different than the world before the crisis. It is our hope that this report will help shape the debate, not just about how to return the world to robust growth, not just about how to prevent a recurrence of another such event, but also how to create a new globalization with better, more democratic governance, one in which there will be greater stability and faster growth, and in which the fruits of that growth are more equitably shared.

Joseph E. Stiglitz
January 2010

FOREWORD

On June 26, 2009, an extraordinary event occurred: the 192 Member States of the United Nations adopted by consensus a broad and exceptionally substantive statement on the World Financial and Economic Crisis and Its Impact on Development. The analysis and recommendations cover the gamut from short-term mitigation to deep structural change, from crisis response to reform of the global economic and financial architecture. The weight of the document is inclined toward agenda setting; it contains few "deliverables" in the form of actionable decisions, but establishes a bold agenda for policy change and institutional development that is broad in scope and profound in its ambitions. Although it is the product, inevitably, of compromise and calculated ambiguity, the Outcome remains the most comprehensive statement issued by any intergovernmental process on the causes and necessary remedies for our world economic crisis.

The Outcome is also a powerful testament to the potential of the United Nations as a forum not only for deliberation, but for decision-making of the highest order—thinking and acting to define the institutional contours of our common lives. It is the result of heroic efforts by a number of individuals and institutions—diplomats and officials, activists and intellectuals in civil society and social movements, and other academic and independent experts from across the globe. The June Outcome draws upon the intellectual capital accumulated during many years of national and regional crises that culminated, after August 2007, in the largest global economic recession since the Great Depression.

The Outcome also reflects the powerful influence of the Commission of Experts on Reform of the International Financial and Monetary System, which I convened under the leadership of Chairman Joseph

Stiglitz, in late November 2008, specifically to assist the Member States of the General Assembly in their deliberations on the world financial and economic crisis. The terms of reference for the Commission were deliberately broad; its focus was shaped by the evolution of the Crisis, by the Commission's own intensive internal deliberations, and through an open, iterative process of dialogue with Member States and other authorities.

Despite its unofficial status, the Commission exerted a powerful pull, its gravitas owing to the reputation and broad representativeness of the Commissioners themselves. The 20 Commissioners came from every region. The cumulative experience that informs their work has to be measured not in decades, but in centuries. They brought to their deliberations a diverse set of lifelong experiences, perspectives, and success as bankers, practitioners, policy-makers and scholars of the first rank. They also brought a willingness to work very hard, and to meet a nearly impossible schedule.

Like the influence of the moon upon the tides, the Commission exercised an enormous influence on the deliberations of the Member States and pulled the debate away from merely superficial concerns and toward the systemic issues whose pernicious impact has become manifest in the present crisis. They helped to embolden thinking by reminding Member States, as they state in the conclusion to this final Report:

> The crisis is not just a once in a century accident, something that just happened to the economy, something that could not be anticipated, let alone avoided. We believe that, to the contrary, the crisis is manmade: It was the result of mistakes by the private sector and misguided and failed policies of the public.

In other words, the Commission members called the UN Member States to take responsibility—but for what, and for and to whom?

∿

Our global economy is broken. This much is widely accepted. But what it is precisely that is broken and needs to be fixed has become a subject of enormous controversy.

In the view adopted by the Commission, and broadly endorsed in the UN Outcome, the crisis we confront is systemic in the deepest sense and has many facets. On this view, the financial crisis that erupted in the United States in September 2009 is the latest and most impactful of several concurrent crises—of food, of water, of energy, and of sustainability—that are tightly interrelated, connected in important ways by an imperious economic perspective that has been implemented, often under duress, across the globe during the last 35 years.

In this perspective, market logic solves nearly all social, economic and political problems. The well-known staples of economic policy complexity such as the need to address economic and non-economic sources of economic instability ("market failure"), the need to account for costs imposed on others and to redress the unfair appropriation of social benefits ("externalities"), the need for public intervention to provide for the conditions and values of sustainable life ("public goods" and "social equity") are all regarded as incidental rather than fundamental issues of economic management.

As the Commission stresses with considerable frequency, the present crisis demonstrates failure at many levels—of theory and philosophy, of institutions, policies and practices, and, less overtly, of ethics and accountability. The essential insight of the report is that our multiple crises are not the result of a failure or failures of the system. Rather, the system itself—its organization and principles, and its distorted and flawed institutional mechanisms—is the *cause* of many of these failures.

It is a habit of contemporary speech to refer to the global economy that we have today as "the economy" and, more insidiously, to present it as a natural phenomenon whose putative laws must be regarded with the same deference as the laws of physics. But, as the enclosed report argues cogently, our global economy is but one of many possible economies, and, unlike the laws of physics, we have a political choice to determine when, where, and to what degree the so-called laws of economic behavior should be allowed to hold sway.

An economy is a man-made ecology, or rather the man-made part of our larger ecology of interaction between the man-made and natural worlds. Together the man-made ecology and the natural ecology sustain—or destroy—the conditions of life. It is essential today, as the UN Outcome and this Report both recognize, to view economic and ecological issues as tightly interrelated, and recognize that our global economic system must be adjusted to the requirements of an era in which the risks engendered by centuries of neglect have reached a point of extreme danger and the costs of adjustment must be borne by the present and succeeding generations. The Commission's Report is forceful on this point: "The conjunction of huge unmet global needs, including responding to global warming and the eradication of poverty, in a world with excess capacity and mass unemployment, is unacceptable."

As the greatest economic philosophers—whose number surely includes Aquinas, Smith, Marx, and Keynes—have all recognized, homo oeconomicus, the acquisitive, emotionally cardboard, and socially atomistic construct of academic economics is a reductio ad absurdum. They did not merely assume that the ethical vocation of human beings should inform their economic decisions and institutions; they insisted on it, and in ways that today are far out of fashion but are also therefore far more necessary today. It is difficult to read this Report and not come to the conclusion that the Commission members share this perspective.

~

One of the most disappointing aspects of the global response to the present crisis has been the almost complete absence of political accountability. While failure has been broad and abundant, corrective action has been comparatively scarce.

In part, perhaps, this owes to the influence of the concept of the present global economy as natural and therefore subject to natural disasters. But under the circumstances that concept is no more than a rhetorical device, an insidious political strategy, of which there are many, to deflect attention and accountability away from the authors of the policies and designers of the institutions that have failed so miserably.

An alternative, complementary explanation is that there is a deep flaw in our system of global economic governance. According to democratic principles those who are deeply affected by a policy should have a say in their formulation, and those who are responsible for massive failures and injury should be held accountable. Our present system of global economic governance does not meet either of these fundamental tests of democratic governance.

The idea that the world community as a whole should become engaged in sorting through the causes and necessary remedies for the world economic crisis has appeared strange to some nations—mostly those few, unsurprisingly, who occupy the most privileged positions in the current institutional arrangement—and deeply necessary to nearly everyone else.

The idea that the United Nations should provide the forum for such engagement appears to be even more polarizing. Throughout the preparatory process for the June Conference, a studious silence was observed in most Northern countries, except for the large number of articles and stories circulated citing unnamed officials and diplomats who decried the very idea of such a UN process as "a joke" and "a farce." The assertion that the UN lacks competency found frequent expression, most notably in the explanation of the vote presented by the U.S. delegate following the adoption of the Outcome: "Our strong view is that the UN does not have the expertise or mandate to serve as a suitable forum or provide direction for meaningful dialogue on a number of issues addressed in the document, such as reserve systems, the international financial institutions, and the international financial architecture."

This view that the United Nations lacks competency to engage on matters of systemic reform received a fatal blow during the intergovernmental consultations (negotiations) that preceded the June Conference. When the lead negotiator for the G7 and China, H.E. Lumumba Di-Aping, proposed to substitute the words "Member States" for the term "United Nations" to name who would be engaged in the process, this small change of words clarified, and settled, the real issue. For no one dared argue that the Member States of the United Nations lack the competency to discuss and make recommendations on the central institutions of our shared global economy and existence.

The United Nations General Assembly, as the world's only legally constituted and globally inclusive intergovernmental body with a clear mandate on economic affairs, has a special and unique role to play in our global deliberations. In part this is because it offers the only forum in which all nations are free to speak and engage on the basis of sovereign equality, and therefore the only forum where those whose voices are least represented in the councils of global economic governance have to be heard and accommodated not as a matter of courtesy but of right. Here alone does the voice of the Global South ring with equal clarity, and here too is where considerations of equity and justice are therefore more likely to be raised.

In matters of global economic governance, the voice of the General Assembly has an additional claim to uniqueness. Owing to the status of the United Nations as the original authority under whose aegis the core institutions of the current architecture were established, and to the role of the General Assembly in particular as its Carter-defined deliberative and constitutive organ, the UN GA is arguably the most important and necessary, if not by any means exclusive, forum for deliberation of global system reform.

~

For the better part of the last year, I have recited the mantra of the world social forum: "A better world is possible." I have also drawn inspiration from the life and teachings of Mahatma Gandhi, who once remarked, "First they ignore you, then they make fun of you, then they fight you, then you win." In Gandhi's vital vision, the fight for social and political change is not reducible to a fight between good and evil, but a struggle for Truth, in which each of us must take personal responsibility in a spirit of love and solidarity, even for those who oppose us and may seek to destroy us.

The Report of the Commission of Experts and the June Outcome are both invitations, perhaps even exhortations, to continue our struggle with truth at and through our United Nations. The UN's imperfections, we must accept, are our imperfections; the responsibility to remake it is ours alone.

I wish to take this opportunity to express my deepest gratitude to Professor Stiglitz and all of the Commissioners whose names are recorded herein, as well as Rapporteur Jan Kregel and my personal representatives, Fr. Francois Houtart and Mr. Ali Boukrami—all of whom approached their work with truly extraordinary dedication and sincerity. Ms. Jill Blackford's efficient administration and wise counsel were indispensable, as were the able editing efforts of Mr. Arjun Jayadev and Mr. Frank Schroeder.

The voluntary support of individuals associated with United Nations Department of Economic and Social Affairs, in particular Drs. Manuel Montes and Richard Kozul-Wright, provided important input to my office early on in the development of this project and at critical stages of work.

I also want to thank the members of my staff, senior advisers Dr. Paul Oquist, Dr. Michael T. Clark, Ambassador Byron Blake, Ambassador Nirupam Sen, and Ambassador Alpo Rusi; the Commission support team led by Deputy Chef de Cabinet Eduardo Mangas, Mr. Luis Nascentes da Silva, Mr. Rachid Ouali, Ms. Claudia Valenzuela, and Ms. Esperanza Escorcia; and indeed all of our colleagues in the Office of the President of the General Assembly, including Ambassador and Chef de Cabinet Norman Miranda and Ambassador and Deputy Chef de Cabinet Sofia Clark, each of whom rolled up their sleeves whenever help was needed to advance a process that literally spanned the globe.

Several governments and institutions also made financial and other in-kind contributions that made the work of the Commission possible. In particular, I wish to express my appreciation for the support of the governments of Algeria, China, Germany, and the Netherlands, without whose timely commitments of financial and political support, it would have been impossible to adhere to the Commission's very aggressive work schedule. The International Parliamentary Union generously offered its facilities for the second full meeting of the Commission in Geneva in March. I want to thank especially, Mr. Anders B. Johnsson, Secretary General, and Ms. Sally-Anne Sader of the IPU, who made the Commission welcome and the meeting productive.

The personal involvement of Minister for Development Cooperation of the Netherlands, H.E. Mr. Bert Koenders, as a host and as a Special Emissary of the President of the General Assembly to Europe was so extensive and effective that he deserves to be considered an emeritus member of the Commission. Mr. Gerben Planting and Ms. Sanne Helderman of the Netherlands Ministry of Foreign Affairs also made important contributions at critical moments.

Together, all have helped us work our way down from the high clouds of mere possibility in order to map the terrain of the real work that lies ahead. They have also provided an example of selfless commitment and hope that I pray will continue and inspire others to join in.

Miguel d'Escoto Brockmann
President of the 63rd Session of the United Nations General Assembly

THE STIGLITZ REPORT

1

INTRODUCTION

THE CRISIS: ITS ORIGINS, IMPACTS, AND THE NEED FOR A GLOBAL RESPONSE

The current financial crisis, which began in the United States, then spread to Europe, has now become global. The rapid spread of the financial crisis from a small number of developed countries to engulf the global economy provides tangible evidence that the international trade and financial system needs to be profoundly reformed to meet the needs and changed conditions of the early 21st century. The crisis has exposed fundamental problems, not only in national regulatory systems affecting finance, competition, and corporate governance, but also in the international institutions and arrangements created to ensure financial and economic stability. These institutions have proven unable to prevent the crisis and have been slow to design and implement adequate responses. Indeed, some policies recommended by these institutions have facilitated the spread of the crisis around the world.

The crisis emanated from the center and reached the periphery. Developing countries, and especially the poor in these countries, are among the hardest hit victims of a crisis they had no role in making. Even emerging-market economies and least-developed countries that have managed their economies well are suffering declining output and employment. Indeed, those countries that have had the best performance in the recent past and that have been most successful in integrating into the global economy have been among the most badly affected.

Past economic crises have had a disproportionate impact on the living standards of the world's poor. Those who are least able to bear these costs will suffer its consequences long after the crisis is over.

Infants who suffer from malnutrition will be stunted for life. Children who drop out of school are not likely to return and will never live up to their potential. Future growth and employment prospects may be impaired if small firms are forced into bankruptcy. Economic policies must be particularly sensitive to these hysteresis effects.

It is important to recognize that what began as a crisis in the financial sector has now become an economic crisis. But, it is not only an economic crisis, it is also a social crisis. According to the International Labour Organization (ILO), some 200 million workers, mostly in developing economies, will be pushed into poverty if rapid action is not taken to counter the impact of the crisis. Even in some advanced industrial countries, millions of households are faced with the threat of losing their homes, their jobs, and access to health care. Economic insecurity and anxiety are increasing among the elderly as much of their life savings disappear with the collapse of asset prices. The ILO estimates that unemployment in 2009 could increase by some 30 million compared with 2007 and reach almost 60 million if conditions continue to deteriorate.

While the crisis began in the financial markets of the advanced industrial countries and then spread to the real economy, in many developing countries, the initial impact of the crisis has been felt in the real sector but is now spreading to (and through) the financial system. Developing countries are being affected through falling export demand and prices, accompanied by reversals of capital flows and reductions in remittances. While developed countries have the fiscal flexibility to respond, to stimulate their economies, to shore up failing financial institutions, to provide credit, and to strengthen social protections, most developing countries have tighter budget constraints, and resources directed towards offsetting the impact of the crisis must be diverted from development purposes. Money spent to extend social protection may be at the expense of future growth.

While it is important to introduce structural changes to adapt the international system to prevent future crises, this cannot be achieved without significant immediate measures to promote recovery from the current crisis. To the extent possible, these measures should promote, or at least be consonant with, the needed long-run structural changes.

At the same time, the international community cannot focus exclusively on immediate measures to stimulate the economy if it wishes to achieve a robust and sustainable recovery. This crisis is, in part, a crisis of confidence, and confidence cannot be restored unless steps are taken to begin the more fundamental reforms required, for instance, through improved regulation of the financial system.

Any solution—short-term measures to stabilize the current situation and long-term measures to make another recurrence less likely—must be global and must pay due attention to impacts on all countries and all groups within society. In particular, the welfare of developed and developing countries is mutually interdependent in an increasingly integrated world economy. Without a truly inclusive response, recognizing the importance of all countries in the reform process, global economic stability cannot be restored, and economic growth, as well as poverty reduction worldwide, will be threatened.

Short-term measures to stabilize the current situation must ensure the protection of the poorest in the least-developed countries, many of whom are in sub-Saharan Africa. As we have noted, the poor countries, and especially the poor within all countries, will bear a heavy burden of adjustment. Long-term measures not only must be designed to make another recurrence less likely, but they also must ensure sustainable financing to strengthen the policy response of developing countries.

Any inclusive global response will require the participation of the entire international community. To respond to this need, the President of the General Assembly created the present Commission of Experts to identify measures needed to respond to the crisis and to recommend longer-term reforms, paying explicit attention to the needs of developing countries. Recognizing work by the G-7/8, G-20 and others, the Commission sees its own work as complementary, seeking to focus on the origins of the crisis as well as the impacts of and responses to the crisis on poverty and development.

Reform of the international system must have, as its goal, the improved functioning of the world's economic system in support of the global good. This entails simultaneously pursuing long-term objectives, such as sustainable and equitable growth, creation of employment in accordance with the "decent work" concept, responsible use of natural resources, reduction of greenhouse gas emissions, and more immediate concerns, including addressing the challenges posed by the food and financial crises and global poverty. As the world focuses on the exigencies of the moment, long-standing commitments to achievement of the internationally agreed development goals, including the Millennium Development Goals and protecting the world against the threat of climate change, must remain overarching priorities; indeed, both the immediate steps taken in response to the crisis and longer-term global reforms should provide an opportunity to accelerate progress toward meeting these goals. While the world will eventually recover from the global economic crisis, the resolution of other challenges, including those posed by introducing new forms of energy to counter global warming, eliminating global poverty, and the potential shortage of food and water, will require additional measures. The conjunction of huge unmet global needs, including responding to the challenges of global warming and the eradication of poverty, in a world with excess capacity and mass unemployment is unacceptable.

Over ten years ago, at the time of the Asian financial crisis, there was much discussion of the necessity for rapid reform of the global financial architecture if the world were to avoid the occurrence of another major crisis. Little—too little, it is now evident—was done. It is imperative to provide an adequate, immediate response to the current crisis, but also to begin the long-run reforms that will be necessary to create a more stable, prosperous and balanced global economy. The aim must be to avoid future global crises.

Both developed and developing countries must recognize that globalization must meet the needs of all citizens of the world. While it promised to help stabilize global financial markets and reduce the scale of domestic economic fluctuations, it failed to do so. Rather, it served to facilitate the spread of contagion from one country to another. A failure in one economy is now leading to a global recession or depression. And unless something is done, and done quickly, those in developing countries are likely to be among the people who suffer most.

This report presents an analytical framework for understanding what has gone wrong and what the possible remedies are. It presents both broad perspectives on policies and specific recommendations. This introductory chapter provides an overview of some of the key issues and policy frameworks and perspectives. As noted, the crisis is both a financial crisis and an economic crisis. It has both macroeconomic and microeconomic aspects. It began as a failure in the financial sector, but the problems in that sector were, in part, a result of underlying macroeconomic problems, such as growing global imbalances and growing income inequalities within and between countries. The fact that existing global institutions did little to prevent the crisis, and then delayed developing adequate responses to the crisis, suggests important institutional problems that the international community needs to address. The frequent crises that have accompanied globalization, with problems in one country quickly spilling over and creating problems in others, suggest the need for reform of the international financial system to meet the needs of an increasingly interdependent world economy. The fact that a major impact of these crises has been on the poor and developing countries makes it clear that there are inadequacies in global market and non-market mechanisms for managing financial risks.

The current economic crisis should provide an opportunity to reassess global economic arrangements and prevalent economic doctrines. Large changes have occurred in the global economy in recent years, e.g., in the sources of global savings, foreign exchange reserves, and GDP, and these are not fully reflected in our global economic institutions and arrangements. In trying to resolve the problems of the short-run crisis, it is important to seize the opportunity to make deeper reforms that enable the world to enter the 21st century with a more equitable and stable global financial system, one which could usher in an era of enhanced prosperity for all countries.

THE INSTITUTIONAL RESPONSES TO THE CRISIS

There have been unprecedented efforts to address the crisis. The stimulus measures introduced by many countries around the world will dampen the impact of the crisis. However, it must be recognized that there can be no return to the *status quo ante*. It is essential that governments undertake reforms that address the underlying factors that contributed to the current economic crisis if the world is to emerge from the crisis into sustainable, balanced growth. It also is essential if there is to be a quick restoration of confidence. Failure to act quickly to address the global economic downturn and more fundamental problems that gave rise to it would increase the depth and duration of the crisis, making it more difficult and more costly to create a balanced and robust recovery.

Most of these longer-term reforms are not just luxuries to be undertaken at leisure once the recovery is assured; they are essential to the recovery itself. Moreover, there is substantial risk that unless work on these more fundamental reforms is undertaken now, momentum for reform will be lost with the recovery. There are strong political forces at play, and those who have benefited from existing arrangements or recent changes will resist fundamental reforms. But allowing these interests to prevail would ensure the recurrence of a crisis. This is one lesson to be learned from the Asian financial crisis of 1997–1998, where relatively quick recovery left the financial system unchanged and helped set the stage for the current crisis.

The urgent need to respond to the crisis has been highlighted by the meetings of the heads of government of the Group of 20 in November 2008 in Washington and in April 2009 in London. These have led to commitments to undertake large fiscal expenditure packages, to introduce significant regulatory reforms, and to provide increased assistance to developing countries. These are important initiatives, but more important is the recognition that the global nature of the crisis means that it cannot be resolved by a small group of advanced industrialized countries and instead must be addressed in a more inclusive framework. Moreover, the actions proposed and the processes by which decisions are made and implemented are not ideal.

First, and most important, the decisions concerning necessary reforms in global institutional arrangements must be made not by a self-selected group (whether the G-7, G-8, G-10, G-20, or G-24), but by all the countries of the world, working in concert. This inclusive global response will require the participation of the entire international community; it must encompass representatives of the entire planet, the G-192.

While proposals from smaller groups will necessarily play an important role in developing a global consensus on key and complex issues, decision-making must reside within international institutions with broad political legitimacy and with adequate representation of both middle-income countries and the least-developed countries. The only institution that has this broad legitimacy today is the United Nations.

Better representation and democratic legitimacy would not require the presence of all countries in all deliberations. Working committees, with representative membership chosen by democratic selection mechanisms and with equitable representativeness, could be limited to a size that would ensure effective decision making and yet also ensure that a wide variety of voices and perspectives are taken into account. The fact that all existing democracies have been able to achieve satisfactory solutions to these problems suggests that they are not irresolvable.

POLICY RESPONSES TO THE CRISIS

Sustainable responses to the crisis require identifying the factors underlying the crisis and the reasons for its rapid spread around the world. There have been policy failures at both the micro- and macro-economic levels. Loose monetary policy, inadequate regulation, and lax supervision interacted to create financial instability. "Reforms" over the past three decades have exposed countries to greater instability and reduced the impact of "automatic" stabilizers. In some countries, social protection has been weakened, with the result that the adverse consequences of major crises, such as the one the world is now facing, have been especially hard on the poor. But any inquiry into the causes and origins of the crisis must go further, examining why these policies were pursued.

At the global level, some international institutions continue to recommend policies, such as financial sector deregulation and capital market liberalization, that are now recognized as having contributed to the creation and rapid diffusion of the crisis. The inadequate responses to the last global crisis in 1997–1998 led to a change in policy frameworks within many developing countries that induced them to hold increasing levels of reserves, which contributed to the large global imbalances whose disorderly unwinding was widely feared as an additional source of financial instability.

The conduct of monetary policy in the United States has been focused on offsetting the potential negative impact on aggregate demand of the real estate crisis at the end of the 1980s and the collapse of the information technology equity bubble at the beginning of the new millennium. It thus acted to support global aggregate demand and contributed to global imbalances that were also aggravated by increasing income inequality in most countries.

In many countries, the focus of monetary policy was on price stability, rather than other factors that might contribute to long-term growth and stability, because it was believed that low inflation was a necessary and (almost) sufficient condition for economic prosperity. It should now be clear that monetary authorities must recognize the consequences of their policy decisions on the stability of asset prices as well as the stability of financial institutions.

Part of the reason for inadequate financial regulation was an inadequate appreciation of the limits of the market mechanism—the prevalence of what economists call "market failures." While such failures arise in many markets, they are particularly important in financial markets and can have disproportionately large consequences as they spill over into "real" economic activity.

The current crisis reflects problems that go beyond the conduct of monetary policy and regulation of the financial sector; it has exposed broader flaws in the understanding of the functioning of markets. There was a widespread belief that unfettered markets are, on their own, quickly self-correcting and efficient.

This suggests that it is necessary to review the policies currently advocated by international institutions—such as the International Monetary Fund, the World Bank, the regional development banks, and the World Trade Organization—as well as many international agreements that are based on these premises.

THE GLOBAL CRISIS NEEDS A GLOBAL RESPONSE

The current crisis may be considered a manifestation of the impact of real and financial externalities. Most visibly, the failure of markets in the financial sector had substantial negative externalities on real output and employment. But more generally, in a globally integrated world, the actions of any one country have effects on others. Too often, these externalities are not taken into account in national policy decisions. Developed countries, in particular, need to be aware of the consequences of these externalities, and developing countries need frameworks to help protect them from regulatory and macroeconomic failures in the major countries. Ironically, much of the effort to coordinate international economic policy has focused on putting constraints on countries whose behavior is not systemically significant, while doing little about countries whose policies can have systemically significant consequences.

Similarly, the importance of externalities is often ignored in the design of countries' policies in response to crises. Presently, there is a risk that countries may undertake insufficient expansionary measures because some of the benefits of their policies (such as deficit-financed expenditures) may accrue to those outside the country. As a result, without global cooperation, countries may spend less than the optimal amount on stimulus packages, as they balance the benefits of the stimulus with the cost of extra debt burdens. Furthermore, they may try to distort their stimulus packages so that more benefits accrue domestically. The net result is that the overall global stimulus impact will be sub-optimal: all may suffer.

The introduction of additional protectionist policies to improve domestic conditions at the expense of trading partners also has negative externalities that will impede the recovery from the crisis. Such beggar-thy-neighbor policies contributed to the depth of the Great Depression. Then, countries attempted to augment the impact of expenditure policies through competitive currency devaluations or restraints on trade such as quotas and tariffs. Such moves proved to be counterproductive. In the current situation, explicit moves in this direction, at least of the magnitude and transparency of those that occurred in the Great Depression, may be unlikely. Nonetheless, more subtle versions of such protectionism are already occurring. It is a matter of concern that although the G-20 resolved not to engage in protectionist measures in their meeting in November 2008, by March 2009, nearly all had broken that pledge. Particularly disturbing are protectionist measures directed against developing countries.

It has long been recognized that subsidies can be just as disturbing to a free and fair trading system as tariffs. They may also be more detrimental to the creation of a level playing field since rich countries have greater resources to implement them. Measures designed to offset the impact of subsidies implemented in developed countries reduce the availability of already scarce development funds. In the current crisis, developed countries have provided unprecedented subsidies, primarily in the form of financial support for domestic financial and non-financial enterprises that developing countries cannot match in breadth and scale. They also produce a less obvious distortion in that the knowledge that firms in advanced industrial countries will be rescued if things go badly gives them a distinct advantage over firms in poorer countries. This highlights the lack of coherence between existing global macroeconomic and financial arrangements, policies, and frameworks and those governing trade. Whether there ever was a level playing field may be debated; that there is no longer one cannot be.

Other measures taken in response to the crisis are implicitly protectionist and may have reinforced the natural response of banks to reduce their lending to developing countries. For example, some international banks that have received support from their home governments may have been encouraged to reduce their lending in developing countries to ensure that domestic lending increases. Or banks that have received large amounts of public money may reduce lending even without explicit governmental oversight because of worries about adverse political reactions. This creates a new dimension of financial market protection that exacerbates long-standing asymmetries in the functioning of global financial markets.

Unless actions are taken to curb financial market and other forms of implicit and explicit protection and to provide developing countries with compensatory payments to offset the possible distortions that may result from the bailouts, guarantees, and asymmetric expansionary fiscal policies, there is a risk that the global inequalities which contributed to the crisis will increase.

A lack of resources is a major impediment to the introduction of strong stimulus packages in developing countries. This report thus calls for a substantial increase in resources available to developing countries, not just to undertake stimulus measures, but to cope with the negative impact of the crisis. Funding to shore up their banking systems, provide credit, including trade credit, and strengthen social protection should be provided, and developing countries should have expanded scope to implement policies that will allow appropriate counter-cyclical policies and to design other structural policies consonant with their needs, objectives, and situation.

Reforming International Economic Institutions

It is apparent that the conditionalities often imposed by international financial institutions in their support of developing countries were counterproductive. The demand that countries implement short-run pro-cyclical policies has exacerbated downturns, while long-run structural policies exposed countries to greater risk and undermined social protection. It is important to design reforms that prevent, or at least reduce the likelihood of, such counterproductive policies in the future. Part of the answer is to be found in the reform of the governance of international economic institutions.

SOME BASIC PRINCIPLES

In addressing the crisis, several other basic principles—besides, for instance, acting with all due speed, recognizing the necessity to offset new forms of externalities, and avoiding financial and other types of protectionism—should guide the responses of the international community.

Restoring Balance Between Market and Government

The crisis is, in part, a result of excessive deregulation of financial markets. Restoring the global economy to health will require restoring to the state the appropriate role of regulator of financial markets. In addition, the externalities associated with both the global economic crisis and the global climate crisis can be addressed only by restoring government to its appropriate role in providing collective action at the national and the global levels.

Greater Transparency and Accountability

Greater transparency in responding to the crisis is necessary. More generally, democratic principles, including inclusive participation in decision-making, should be strengthened and respected. Regrettably, in responding to the crisis, many governments have undertaken non-transparent actions and relied heavily on central banks, with only limited democratic accountability. Some central banks with only limited direct accountability have introduced measures—without parliamentary or congressional approval—in support of financial institutions that have exposed taxpayers to massive risks.

Short-Run Actions Consistent with Long-Run Visions

In taking policy actions, it is imperative that governments not exacerbate the current crisis through actions that have adverse impacts on other countries or result in structural changes that increase future instability or reduce future growth. For example, in some countries, the response to the crisis created by excessive risk undertaken by financial institutions that were too big to fail has resulted in bank consolidation, which increases such risks in the future.

Assessing Distributive Impacts

Any economic policy, including those responding to crises, has large distributive consequences, both within and between countries, and policy makers need to be attentive to those consequences. As noted, previous financial and economic crises have had particularly adverse effects on poverty, but the strategies employed to address them have sometimes resulted in exacerbating income and wealth inequalities. Bank bailouts and restructurings have played a particularly important role in these adverse redistributions of income and wealth. For example, the unprecedented lowering of interest rates may have been the correct macroeconomic response to the crisis, but it has produced a sharp reduction in the incomes of retirees who did not gamble on risky securities and invested prudently in short- or medium-term government securities. In the East Asian crisis, by contrast, high interest rates were imposed as a condition for international assistance. Small businesses that found themselves unable to bear the burden of debt were forced into bankruptcy.

Avoiding an Increase in Global Imbalances and Asymmetries

There are large inequalities in the global economy and large asymmetries in the global economic framework. It is important that the measures introduced to respond to this crisis seek to reduce, not exacerbate, these inequalities and asymmetries. For instance, in a crisis counter-cyclical policies are pursued by developed countries, while most developing countries pursue pro-cyclical policies. As noted, this is a result of both the limited availability of resources to engage in counter-cyclical policies, and the restrictions on "policy space" resulting from conditions imposed on countries seeking assistance from international institutions. But even if all countries apply similar policies, the policies can have asymmetric effects: guarantees provided to financial institutions in developed countries cannot be effectively matched by developing countries. These asymmetries, especially in the absence of adequate mechanisms for transferring and mitigating risk, impose high costs on developing countries, increasing volatility and reducing growth.

Distribution and Incidence of Risk

All economic policies involve risks and uncertainties, but under different economic policies, different groups may bear the brunt of this risk. An aggressive stimulus policy may, for instance, increase the risk of inflation from over-stimulation, and those with long-term investments with fixed nominal returns (such as bondholders) may suffer. A weak stimulus may lead to prolonged unemployment, with workers suffering.

Irreversibilities (Hysteresis Effects)

Policies need to be sensitive to non-linearities and problems of irreversibilities. Some policy mistakes are easy to correct, others are not. It may be easier to damp down demand in an economy that faces a risk of overheating than to resuscitate a dying economy, just as it may be easier to dampen nascent inflation than to tame hyperinflation. Reversing policies that have led to the bankruptcy of a firm cannot bring it back to life. An economy may be able to absorb small shocks, but large shocks can have disproportionately adverse effects. These simple maxims of risk management need to be borne in mind in designing responses to the crisis.

Intellectual Diversity

While much of the support for globalization and the changes in economic policy (e.g., in deregulation) over the past quarter century may have been driven by particular interests, it was also premised on economic doctrines whose theoretical foundations and empirical bases were, at best, questionable. Modern economic theory has brought into question many of the ideas underlying market fundamentalism, including the notion that unregulated markets lead to efficient outcomes or that markets are self-regulating and stable. The current economic crisis has raised further questions concerning these doctrines and has highlighted the relevance of alternative theories and ideas. Any approach to addressing the current economic crisis and preventing future episodes must be robust, in the sense that the conclusions and policy prescriptions cannot rely on economic doctrines in which there is, or should be, limited confidence. Some international institutions have advocated notions of competitive pluralism, encouraging the creation of a marketplace of ideas, while others have tried to enforce a single-minded adherence to a particular ideology that the crisis has shown to be inadequate. Strengthening the diversity of ideas may contribute both to global stability and to a strengthening of democracy.

The crisis also highlights that the standard policy nostrums—that countries should have sound macroeconomic policies, strong governance, transparency, and good institutions—may be less than helpful. Countries that held themselves out as models of best practices have been shown to have had deeply flawed macroeconomic policies and institutions and to have suffered from major shortfalls in transparency.

IMPACT ON DEVELOPING COUNTRIES

The crisis is likely to extract a particularly high toll on developing countries for four reasons.

First, the citizens of these countries have fewer resources with which to cope with a crisis of this magnitude.

Secondly, they already suffer from a lack of automatic stabilizers due to the embryonic nature of their fiscal and social protection systems.

Third, the limited ability to borrow in international financial markets may impose constraints on their ability to pursue counter-cyclical fiscal and monetary policies. Many countries are forced, for instance, to pursue pro-cyclical fiscal policies because tax revenues decline in a downturn and they cannot find adequate financing for existing, let alone expanded, government expenditures. In this crisis especially, many firms and countries will face credit constraints and higher borrowing costs because capital flows to developing countries are likely to be markedly lower and risk premiums have increased substantially. To retain foreign investors, countries may be tempted to raise interest rates, with adverse effects on the real economy. But as in the East Asian and global financial crises, such interest rate increases may not have the desired stabilizing impact and may instead reduce economic growth and, as the economy slows, erode confidence and cause capital outflows. It is possible that the risk-adjusted interest rate may even fall as the nominal interest rate is increased.

Fourth, these ever-present threats have been exacerbated by financial market integration. Countries that have fully opened their capital accounts, have engaged in financial market liberalization, and have relied on private finance from international capital markets are among those likely to be most adversely affected. Many countries have come to rely on foreign banks, some from countries that were poorly regulated and followed inappropriate macroeconomic policies and that now find their capital badly impaired. These institutions are now repatriating capital, with adverse effects on developing countries. The difficulty is compounded by the fact that many developing countries have entered into free trade agreements (FTAs), bilateral investment treaties (BITs) and World Trade Organization commitments that enshrine the policies of market fundamentalism noted above and further limit their ability to regulate financial institutions and instruments, manage capital flows, or protect themselves from the effects of financial market protectionism.

In the past, those developing countries that have accessed IMF financing have been constrained by international financial institutions to adopt restrictive policies in times of slow growth or even recession. Such pro-cyclical policies are counterproductive, since one of the purposes of assistance should be to enable developing countries to stabilize their economies. But in the current global crisis it is not just the developing countries that are forced to adopt such policies that suffer; the entire global economy suffers. International responses require all countries to engage in expansionary policies—*including developing countries.* The purpose of IMF assistance should be, in part, to enable the developing countries to participate in this global effort. Even without these artificially imposed constraints, the natural market constraints referred to earlier may impede developing countries, even those receiving assistance, from having counter-cyclical policies as strong as would be desirable.

The legacy of past imposition of pro-cyclical policies may itself exert a depressing effect on developing countries today, unless there are strong and clear signals of a marked change in the policy regime. These countries may have to pay higher risk premiums in the current crisis as market participants know that they are likely to face a deeper and longer downturn than they would have had they been allowed to pursue more counter-cyclical policies. Unfortunately, the signals are mixed: constraints on implementing counter-cyclical policies have become apparent in the current crisis in the conditions attached to IMF programs in several countries.

More broadly, developing country dependence on IMF financing has constricted policy space for counter-cyclical policy. Concerns about future imposition of these constraints have contributed to several countries building reserves and global imbalances. Unless the policy regime is changed, incentives for further build-up of reserves could increase, impairing the ability of the global economy to emerge quickly from the global economic crisis.

If appropriate measures are not taken quickly by the international community, developing countries may, in fact, be hurt rather than helped by the responses of developed countries to the crisis. In the short- and medium-term, it is necessary that developing countries undertake a variety of counter-cyclical policies—including social protection measures, infrastructure development, and credit guarantees—and it is imperative that developed countries provide them with appropriate assistance and policy space to do this. Such measures may also ensure fair global competition.

The major focus of this report is on short-term measures and the longer-term reforms of the international financial system that support the developing countries and their aspirations for development. As noted above, developing countries will bear the greatest costs of the crisis but do not have the resources necessary to deal with its negative impacts. Measures are needed very quickly to avoid further deepening of the crisis in emerging and developing countries, including restoring and expanding social protection and reducing the pro-cyclical features of economic policy. Delay will mean that the eventual cost of dealing with the problem will be higher, and the length and depth of the downturn will be greater, with more innocent victims losing their jobs, with more small—and even large—businesses forced into bankruptcy, and with public finances increasingly put in jeopardy. The consequences of our current failures may be felt for decades to come.

This report presents its analysis and recommendations in the following four chapters. Chapter 2 deals with the macro issues and perspectives lying behind the crisis and the measures that need to be taken to overcome it. Chapter 3 deals with the causes of instability in the financial system in particular and impact on the overall economic system, as well as those measures that should be taken to ensure financial stability at the level of individual financial institutions and at the systemic level. In Chapter 4 the report assesses the adequacy of existing international institutions, how they should be reformed, and new institutions that could be created to make the system more stable and better able to serve the needs of developing countries. Finally, Chapter 5 deals with International Financial Innovations, those measures that might be introduced to what is called the international financial architecture to meet the needs of the globalized world of the 21st century.

2

MACROECONOMIC ISSUES
AND PERSPECTIVES

While the current economic crisis is global in its causes and ramifications, the responses to the crisis have been decided and implemented at the national level. Little attention has been given to the global externalities and spillovers that arise out of those uncoordinated decisions. The challenge raised by the crisis is to design a framework and road map for a coordinated, global response that recognizes the differing constraints facing individual countries, particularly the most vulnerable developing countries.

Coordination is essential to the success of the different actions currently being implemented by governments in response to the crisis because the impact of individual policies will depend on actions undertaken by other countries. It is important that national governments recognize that their policies will be more effective in protecting their citizens from the crisis if they are internationally coordinated.

Failure to coordinate policies can lead to growing global imbalances and increased exchange rate and asset price volatility, which will impair a return to robust and sustainable growth. Protectionist measures introduced in response to the crisis would impede the speed of global recovery.

National policies introduced in response to the crisis may have unintended and unforeseen protectionist effects. While measures such as guarantees and bailouts may not be intended to provide trade protection, they may nonetheless create advantages restricted to domestic firms. Thus, it is important to design measures that protect domestic residents without increasing trade protection. It is also necessary to find ways of extending social protection without such protectionism. One major lesson of the Great Depression is that certain forms of protection are likely to be counterproductive. In current conditions, the effects of protectionism may be even worse because of the increased global integration of trade and production.

Developing countries and other emerging markets are more exposed to these adverse effects. A globally "balanced" response to the crisis will require both coordination of national recovery programs and, because many developing countries do not have the requisite resources, a substantial increase in official assistance to developing countries.

The objectives of national and international policy should be a quick recovery and protection of vulnerable populations, who are likely to be the most adversely affected, and in ways that promote equitable, democratic, environmentally and socially sustainable development. It should, at the same time, facilitate the necessary restructuring of national economies and the global economic system.

SOURCES OF THE CRISIS

There have been many failures behind the current financial crisis. Chapter 3 of this report analyzes regulatory failures in developed country financial systems and management of risk. But macroeconomic failures were part of other failures. It is important to understand these interrelationships in order to design policies that will allow the global economy to emerge from the crisis with more robust growth and to make recurrence of crisis less likely.

The sub-prime mortgage crisis, which led to a wider crisis in credit markets, was partly caused by an "excess" supply of liquidity in global capital markets and the failures of the central banks in the United States and some other advanced industrial countries to act to restrain liquidity and dampen the speculative increases in housing and other asset prices. While lax financial regulation may have contributed to the particular *form* taken by the crisis, the magnitude of this excess liquidity, and other associated factors, made further difficulties likely.

While problems initially appeared in the financial sector, the origins of the problem were deeper and cannot be addressed *simply* by repairing the "plumbing" of the financial sector. For example, the rise of income inequalities discussed below and inadequacies in competition policy and corporate governance, discussed in Chapter 3, were of major significance.

Focusing attention on public policy failures should not, however, divert attention from underlying market failures. Financial markets mismanaged risk and misallocated capital. Had markets done what they should have, the availability of capital at low cost could have led to large increases in productivity, rather than further impoverishing lower income Americans.

The similarities between this crisis and several other financial and economic crises, including the Great Depression, suggest that economic policies have not fully taken into account the lessons of those crises. Part of the reason for this lies in economic doctrines that became fashionable in some quarters during the last three decades.

As the international community frames an immediate response to the crisis, it would be a mistake to forget this broader context. The present chapter thus focuses on macroeconomics—both the underlying macroeconomic problems and the necessary macroeconomic policy responses that will make for a speedy recovery and make recurrence of the crisis less likely.

Role of Economic Doctrines

Part of the explanation of the current crisis may be found in the underlying economic fundamentals. Another is in the economic theories that motivated the financial and economic policies that produced the crisis. A more detailed discussion of the impact of these economic doctrines on regulatory policy is found in Chapter 3. These same economic doctrines—the belief that economic agents are rational, that governments are inherently less informed and less motivated by sound economic principles and therefore their interventions are likely to distort market allocations, and that markets are efficient and stable, with a strong ability to absorb shocks—also affected macroeconomic policies.

One of the most important lessons of the Great Depression was that markets are not self-correcting and that government intervention is required at the macroeconomic level to ensure recovery and a return to full employment. In the aftermath of the Great Depression, governments introduced policies that provided automatic stabilizers for aggregate demand and implemented discretionary policy frameworks to reduce economic instability. But as the Great Depression and earlier panics and crises faded from memory, confidence in the self-stabilizing nature of the market returned.

The fact that the world recovered so quickly from financial crises such as the East Asian crisis of 1997–1998 and the global liquidity crisis of August 1998 induced false confidence in the self-correcting nature of market processes. While the recovery was due to public policies, it was credited to market processes. More generally, the historical role of government intervention in recovery and stability was forgotten.

Changes in the Global Economy

The level of international economic interdependence may also have contributed to an increase in vulnerability of the global economic system to external shocks that produce larger negative impacts on global aggregate demand.

In some countries, the weakening of social protection and the reduced progressivity of income tax systems weakened the automatic stabilizers. In some countries, structural changes within the market had similar consequences. Too often in national policy discourse, and even in some theoretical discussion, globalization was used as a pretext for ostensibly competitive reductions in social protection, creating a global race to the bottom.

Constraints imposed in the European Union by the Stability and Growth Pact and concerns in other countries about the size of fiscal deficits and national debt may impair the use of counter-cyclical fiscal policies to respond effectively to shocks, including the extraordinary shock the world faces today.

The expansion in lending associated with new risk management practices, deregulation, and accommodating monetary policy allowed consumption to grow more rapidly than incomes. However, this support for aggregate demand in the face of rising income and wealth inequality came at the costs of increasing household indebtedness to unsustainable levels. Moreover, policies in many developing countries aimed at reducing external constraints led to ever-increasing global imbalances. In some of these countries these policies and the trade surplus to which they led were a defense against international financial volatility.

Growing Inequality As a Source of the Crisis

Although economic globalization has supported rapid increases in GDP, the real increases in societal wealth were smaller because of growing environmental damage, which took a significant but largely overlooked toll. Globalization has also produced increased volatility in incomes and increasing income inequality. It has been associated with increasing inequality of income not only within developing countries but also among developing countries and between developed and many developing countries. Inequality has also increased within developed countries. When combined with changes in financial markets, this growth in inequality has had important consequences for the evolution and resolution of the crisis.

It is now recognized that in most advanced industrial countries, median wages stagnated during the last quarter century, while income inequalities surged in favor of the upper quintiles of the income distribution. In effect, money was transferred from those who would have spent to meet basic needs to those who had far more than they could easily spend, thus weakening aggregate effective demand.

There were many forces contributing to this growth in inequality, including asymmetric globalization, especially that facilitated the greater ease of the movement of capital than of labor, the weakening of labor unions, deficiencies in corporate governance, and a breakdown of social conventions which resulted in greater disparities in compensation between top executives and other workers. Finally, it was believed that increasing after-tax remuneration and providing other economic incentives, like non-monetary benefits, would increase savings, labor supply, investment, and thus growth. These problems were exacerbated by the reduction of progressivity in tax structures in some countries. In most OECD countries, the tax rate for the highest tax bracket has been reduced by more than 10 percentage points on average.

The negative impact of stagnant real incomes and rising income inequality on aggregate demand was largely offset by financial innovation in risk management and lax monetary policy that increased the ability of households to finance consumption by borrowing, especially in the United States and some other developed countries such as the United Kingdom. On the other hand the search for yield by the higher income classes to invest their increased incomes supported the formation of asset bubbles. But increasing household indebtedness was not sustainable. Or rather, what was perceived to be sustainable was dependent on artificially inflated asset prices that created the illusion that household wealth was increasing at a faster pace than their debt. The support for the bubble thus depended on expansionary monetary policy together with financial sector innovation leading to ever-increasing asset prices that allowed the households virtually unlimited access to credit.

It is possible to argue that the increase in public debt in some OECD countries was partly the consequence of the evolution of the distribution of income. In some advanced countries such as those in the European Union, social protection systems that provided partial compensation for stagnating income in a context of high unemployment were financed through increased public deficits and public debt.

In countries where the social protection system is much weaker (e.g., the US), increased household borrowing may have postponed a decline in living standards and consumption in tandem with the decline in real wages.

The 2001 and 2003 tax cuts in the United States provided little stimulus to the economy but had a negative impact on government deficit and debt, reducing the room for fiscal policy measures to deal with rising unemployment and placing a greater burden on monetary policy.

The Iraq War and other events that helped increase the price of oil had a further depressing effect on countries that import energy, including the U.S. The magnitude of the increase in energy prices was exacerbated by financial speculation. This change in the price of energy, accompanied by government support of the production of bio fuels, contributed to higher food prices. The sharp increase in energy prices thus directly and indirectly brought further reductions in purchasing power in many countries. Since a large fraction of low income households' budgets are spent on energy and food this further increased income inequality. Moreover the transfer of income, from those who suffered from these price increases to those who benefited, weakened global aggregate demand and contributed to the global imbalances that played an important role in the crisis.

While the negative impact of income inequality and energy, commodity, and food inflation on global aggregate demand was thus temporarily offset by mounting private and public debt, it should be clear that this was not sustainable. But those responsible for macroeconomic management, including the monetary authorities, failed to recognize this and to take appropriate actions.

Policy responses designed to ensure a robust and sustainable recovery from this crisis must address the question of how growing inequality of income and wealth might be reversed. Should the trend towards reducing the progressivity of the fiscal system be reversed? Capital mobility in the absence of tax harmonization among countries has contributed to tax competition, undermining the ability of governments to impose taxes on capital. Should some harmonization of business taxation throughout the world be advocated? Are there ways of directing public attention to inequality—which in turn might translate into public action? Should, for instance, changes in inequality in each country become public knowledge through a yearly parliamentary debate?

One thing seems to be certain: the use of fiscal advantages to attract foreign investors that has become common with the globalization of production is not sustainable for at least two reasons. The first is that it contributes directly to the rise in inequality through a regressive redistribution of income; the second is the indirect rise of inequality that results from the reduced capacity of governments to provide public goods to the population.

Global Imbalances and Imbalances in Global Aggregate Demand

Part of the reason the United States was able to sustain an expanding external deficit was the decision of many emerging market countries in Asia and Latin America to respond to the financial crises in the 1990s by adopting policies to strengthen their external balances. As some other emerging market countries chose deliberately an export-led growth strategy, the resulting increase in foreign exchange reserves, along with the increasing reserves accruing to oil-producing countries from higher oil prices, were invested in official dollar assets and provided the financial counterpart to the rising US external deficits.

The apparently unending increase in what came to be known as global imbalances raised concerns that they were unsustainable and that their disorderly reversal might generate a global financial disruption or exchange rate crisis. But those responsible for global macroeconomic management did not take appropriate action.

There were several reasons why many emerging markets strengthened their external accounts, so much so that foreign reserves had grown to $4.5 trillion by October 2008. The first was to prepare a defense against instability due to volatile external financial flows. Countries with insufficient reserves had paid high economic and political costs in the East Asia and global liquidity crises at the end of the previous decade. The loss of economic sovereignty associated with the imposition of pro-cyclical macroeconomic conditionality (as well as other forms of conditionality) as part of International Monetary Fund support programs has also been a source of particular concern to many countries. In addition, some countries had adopted exchange rate stabilization as part of their policies to ensure external balance and stability; some of these countries built up substantial reserves as a result of attempts to prevent exchange rate appreciation, with its adverse effects on economic development (as discussed further in Chapter 5).

Moreover, many developing countries, especially those deriving export incomes from the sale of primary commodities, benefited from rising prices due to rising global growth that accompanied the credit expansion before the crisis. Speculative activity in recent years may also have contributed to rising prices. But, this beneficial trend in prices was also accompanied by increased volatility. Many countries reacted by increasing their prudential reserves during periods of rising prices. These reserves have provided a useful cushion as prices have declined after the outbreak of the crisis.

The collapse of the U.S. mortgage market and the accompanying decline in house prices have produced a sharp increase in household saving and a decline in investment in the US. Other countries had real estate bubbles which also collapsed, with similar consequences. These difficulties in the real estate sector precipitated problems in financial markets, discussed more extensively in the next chapter. The problems of bad lending were aggravated by high leverage and other risky behavior, as well as by a lack of transparency. The resulting collapse of credit reinforced the underlying weakening of aggregate consumption, leading to a rapid decline in global aggregate demand. Declines in final demand as well as increasing cost and decreasing availability of credit led to inventory adjustments which accelerated downward movement in global GDP. But it is important to note that while the inventory adjustments may have aggravated the crisis, they are not part of the underlying cause. Thus, the downturn will not end even when these inventory adjustments are completed; there will be no automatic economic recovery.

Indeed, unless there is a coordinated policy response to this crisis that supports global demand, it is possible that the problem of global imbalances may be exacerbated. With countries facing the threat of high volatility in export earnings and global financial flows, it is rational for countries to increase precautionary savings to protect against future potential calamities. While it is rational for individual countries to "ensure" against another crisis through the build-up of external surpluses and foreign reserves, doing so weakens global aggregate demand. The absence of alternative means for self-protection may not only impair a robust and sustainable recovery, but also lead, in the long run, to further instability. The implication is that a reform of the Global Reserve Currency System that provides an acceptable means of risk mitigation is imperative. Proposals for how this may be done are made in Chapter 5.

It is important that the international community address not only the issue of risk mitigation but also the underlying sources of volatility and the mechanisms by which a financial crisis in one country gives contagion to others. Commodity price speculation, as already noted, probably contributed to the magnitude of price volatility. Reforms in the global financial system, particularly capital and financial market liberalization, have facilitated international contagion and thereby increased the risk of volatility originating from abroad.

Instability and Built-in Destabilizers

Another major source of concern is the limited ability of the economic system to respond to shocks. As noted above, economic systems may have become more unstable as a result of weakening both public and private automatic stabilizers through the reduced progressivity of tax structures, weakening of safety nets, greater wage flexibility, and the movement from defined- benefit to defined-contribution schemes for workers' retirement accounts. New bank regulations, including mark-to-market accounting, may actually have created built-in destabilizers.

An important part of the response to the crisis should therefore be the strengthening of the automatic stabilizers and, more broadly, the adoption of policies that not only reduce the shocks to which economies are exposed but that also dampen the impacts. Strengthening automatic stabilizers will also contribute to the long-term sustainability of growth by reducing the risk associated with income volatility. Chapter 3 discusses one important reform: counter-cyclical capital adequacy and provisioning standards.

Unmanaged flexible exchange rate regimes may expose developing countries to high levels of volatility, especially when combined with certain monetary policies. Countries that raised their interest rates in response to high food and energy prices saw large appreciations of their currency; this has now been followed by large depreciations. Such volatility exacts a heavy toll on developing countries.

INTERNATIONAL RESPONSES: FISCAL POLICY

The Need for and the Nature of a Globally Coordinated Response

This crisis is different from the financial crisis of 1997–1998. Then, the affected countries used exchange rate adjustments and other policies to export their way out of the crisis. In a global crisis affecting all countries, this solution is not possible. It is thus imperative that all countries take strong, coordinated actions to stimulate their economies.

There will be some temptation for countries, especially those with small, open economies, to avoid taking action and benefiting from the expansion that will result from stimulus policies introduced in other countries. As countries balance the trade-off of the benefits of expansion against the costs of increased debt-financed government spending, the risk is that they will undertake insufficient action (when viewed from a global perspective) and, as a result, the global stimulus will be deficient. If all countries think in this way, the global downturn will be more prolonged. Furthermore, when the recovery occurs, it will be more fragile because of an unsustainable distribution of public debts among countries. Hence rapid and sustainable recovery depends on there being no free riders.

Moreover, countries will look for those forms of expenditure that have the largest domestic multipliers. What is at stake is illustrated by the fact that national expenditure multipliers are generally believed to be around 1.5, due to leakages of demand abroad through increased imports. But from a global perspective, there can be no such leakages (though multipliers will still be limited by savings), so that multipliers for a coordinated global expansion are, in reality, much larger.

The implication is that a global crisis requires a global stimulus—it is much like a global public good. The desirable level of the global stimulus is greater than the level that would be implemented by each country thinking only of itself. Moreover, if every country attempts to maximize the domestic impact of its stimulus policies (for example by limiting expenditure on imports), the domestic and the global effectiveness of the policies, measured by the expansionary impact per dollar spent, will be reduced.

Similarly, there will be a temptation in many countries to maximize the domestic impact of their stimulus policy expenditures by introducing protectionist measures that limit leakages of demand into imports from foreign countries. Such measures are more likely to be introduced if countries perceive that others are free riding on their efforts. While these measures may be introduced with the best of intentions, to maximize social protection, they may not respect equal treatment trade principles and, when imitated by others, are likely to be counterproductive. The fact that so many countries have already introduced such protectionist measures should be viewed as a cause of concern. But even measures not designed to have protectionist effects may do so, as noted below. These protectionist measures, both when they are intentional and when they are unintentional, can be particularly harmful to developing countries.

There would be additional benefits from a globally coordinated fiscal response if significant proportions of these expenditures are directed at addressing global problems.

The Need for Stronger Social Protection

Social protection is not only an instrument of social justice but also a major tool of economic stabilization. Well-designed social protection systems make the economy more resilient to shocks by increasing the size of automatic stabilizers. Social protection systems have two components. The first is insurance against risks. It enables smoothing of disposable income, while the enhanced security is of value in its own right. The second component is progressive redistribution, to avoid exclusion and to prevent individuals from being trapped in poverty. Social mobility ("giving to my children better opportunities than I had") is one of the engines of growth and prosperity. But social mobility is all the more likely when "counters are reset," at least partially, at each generation. One of the roles of social systems is a transfer of resources that helps reduce inequalities of initial conditions for each new generation.

Besides its role as "insurance" against income and consumption fluctuations, especially for poorer households, social spending has a more direct impact. Increasing the supply of public goods would free part of the income that is now saved for precautionary purposes and make it available for spending, including investment in both physical infrastructure and human resources. In other words, social spending could "crowd in" private investment and raise the economy's current and future growth rates while decreasing its volatility.

MONETARY POLICY AND RESTRUCTURING FINANCIAL MARKETS

It is equally important that monetary policy be coordinated across countries. In the absence of coordination there may be large, costly, and destabilizing exchange rate movements. But it may be difficult to achieve the necessary level of coordination, given different circumstances and views of the role and objectives of monetary policy. Conventional monetary policy measures to combat the crisis appear to have been exhausted in several major countries. Interest rates in the U.S. and some other countries cannot go much lower. This is one reason why most of the burden of the economic policy response to the crisis must now fall on the shoulders of fiscal policy.

Monetary policy operates by increasing the availability of money and credit and easing the terms at which credit is available. Credit availability is mediated mostly through the banking and financial system. Providing more liquidity to financial institutions may not, however, lead to more lending. A kind of liquidity trap can arise in circumstances such as those the world is facing today. Banks that have seen large erosions in their net worth and that face the prospect of high default rates on existing risky loans are not disposed to increase lending. There may, of course, be overreaction: an episode of excessive risk taking may be followed by an episode of excessive precaution. If that is the case, governments may need to take a more active role in absorbing some of the risk of lending. Chapter 5 discusses some ways in which this may be done.

It is thus probable that traditional monetary policy, by itself, will have only limited effects in resuscitating the global economy; a reduction in interest rates will have an insufficient impact on aggregate demand unless there is an expectation of increased levels of activity and profits.

Monetary policy has traditionally focused on the overnight interest rate at which banks borrow from each other or from the central bank at the discount window. The spread between the policy interest rate and the interest rate at which firms or households can borrow in the medium and long term is an endogenous variable which may actually increase as the policy rate falls. This may be because of changed inflationary expectations or because other changes in the economy result in heightened risk perceptions for lenders. It is possible for monetary authorities to influence longer-term interest rates for government securities and private sector liabilities by opening the discount window to them or by buying them outright through open market purchases. However, this would require the central banks to assume risks beyond those that they have assumed in normal times through their lender-of-last-resort function. It is important that when central banks assume such risks they estimate the future actuarial cost carefully and, to the extent possible, that those costs are reflected in the public domain.

When policy intervention involves the purchase of the liabilities of particular private sector issuers, this may be equivalent to an implicit subsidy on the financing costs for that sector. If it is restricted to some very large firms, it may place other, especially small and medium-sized firms, at a disadvantage.

In the interests of transparency and accountability, since the costs of these actions may have an impact on resource allocation as well as on the balance sheet and the receipts of the national treasury, it is desirable that these decisions be ratified by parliament. This does not imply that central bank independence should be limited. It is the simple recognition that central bank operations that have fiscal consequences should be subject to the same surveillance as treasury operations.

At the same time, it needs to be recognized that traditional prudential policies may also have significant impacts on credit availability and the terms on which it is available. There is a fundamental difference between prudential policies affecting a single bank and those that affect an entire banking system. The introduction of prudential regulations, such as increasing collateral requirements in response to financial difficulties has, in the past, produced excessive credit contraction. While getting the balance right is extraordinarily difficult, central bankers need to be attentive to the macroeconomic consequences of prudential policies. On the other hand, if a policy of forbearance is adopted, it must be accompanied by increased supervision to offset the possibility of moral hazard leading to excessive risk-taking and fraudulent behavior.

In some economies, both conventional and unconventional monetary policies are actively being used to prevent a deepening of the financial crisis and its harmful impacts on employment and income. Part of this is in response to the fact that capital markets have proved inefficient, and these policies are a direct response to such inefficiencies. Nevertheless, as a result of the actions of central banks, there is concern among some observers about high rates of inflation in the short to medium term. While trade-offs between preventing downturns and causing inflation will differ from country to country, at the current juncture, there is a need for global coordination of expansionary policy. In the future, when the current severe crisis appears mitigated, governments and central banks will have to make the difficult decision as to whether and how to retract liquidity. This will certainly depend on the particular context of the country and will require careful balancing of the risks of a return to recession versus accelerating inflation. However, in present conditions the balance of risks appears to be clearly on the side of deflation rather than inflation.

BAILOUTS

Bailouts of financial and non-financial institutions have become a distinguishing feature of the macroeconomic policy responses to this crisis. They have changed expectations of the future development of global financial markets. The efficiency of the bailouts will affect the pace of recovery, the level of the national debt, and the ability of a country to pursue a broader range of objectives. One important goal of the bailouts should be to facilitate a restructuring of the financial sector in ways that enhance economic stability and growth. Bailout decisions must be made with the future design of the financial structure in mind. The financial system of the future must avoid the structural flaws revealed in the recent crisis. In many countries, the financial system had grown too large; it had ceased to be a means to an end and had become an end in itself. The bailouts must be designed to facilitate the restructuring of the financial system, strengthening its capacity to perform its basic functions, including providing finance for small and medium sized enterprises.

The primary concern in this report is the impact of these policies on developing countries and the impact of badly structured bailouts in diverting capital resources from developing countries, impeding their long-term growth prospects. For developing countries especially, the new global financial system should provide better risk management than in the past and provide a more stable source of funding, including funding for small and medium-sized enterprises. In the past, the global financial system has exacerbated economic fluctuations in many developing countries by providing funds in a pro-cyclical manner. It also diverted funds away from lending to small and medium-sized enterprises and forced developing countries to bear a large fraction of the risks they face, including those associated with exchange rate and interest rate fluctuations.

In assessing the policies introduced in response to the crisis, distinctions need to be made among the various impacts on the economy. The primary focus of any bailout is to restore credit flows to the real economy and to contribute to macroeconomic recovery. However, there are distributional impacts of a bailout, and its design will affect stakeholders—equity shareholders, bondholders, workers, firms and households seeking credit—in different ways. There is concern that in some countries there has been excessive focus on saving bankers, bank shareholders, and bondholders instead of on protecting taxpayers and greater focus on saving financial institutions than on resuming credit flows.

One result is that the bailouts have been more costly than they might otherwise have been; another is that the bailouts have been viewed to be very unfair. A third result is that there has been a massive redistribution of wealth from ordinary taxpayers to those bailed out. A bank at risk of being unable to meet its obligations to depositors can be restructured by forcing unsecured debt holders to restructure their claims, diminishing debt and converting the residual into equity. Alternatively, taxpayers can finance a bailout. The latter approach, by subsidizing bondholders who did not have explicit guarantees, may serve to strengthen problems of moral hazard in the future, undermining incentives of those providing credit to engage in due diligence. Because resources are scarce, and the national debt will be larger as a result of a taxpayer financed bailout than it otherwise would have been, there will be less to spend on a stimulus package, on social protection, or on public investments. The perception that the bailouts have been unfair may impede future actions to resuscitate the financial system or to undertake other actions necessary to address the crisis. The fact that the bailouts have, in many cases, been slow to restart lending is of particular concern because if this continues, prospects of a robust recovery are diminished.

Finally, the perception that the bailouts have been unfair may be corrosive to the reputation of the government with longer-term adverse effects. A demoralized body politic that does not believe that government representatives can implement desired change equitably may choose in the future to elect officials who reflect their pessimistic views of the capacity of the public sector to play a constructive role. This would diminish society's capacity to achieve collective responses to many challenges not well-handled by private markets alone.

Given that the focus should be on restarting lending, governments should expand their strategies to include additional options such as the establishment of a new bank or banks operating without the bad debts of the failed institutions and the provision of (partial) guarantees for new lending. The terms on which any newly established banking institution should be provided support should not give the new bank a competitive advantage over existing banks that have not required additional funding. It makes more sense to focus more attention and resources on future growth than on dealing with the mistakes of the past.

In transferring assets and liabilities between the public and private sector, particular attention needs to be given to the prices paid. Overpaying the private sector for a particular asset or bundle of assets represents an unwarranted transfer to the firm at the expense of the taxpayers and an inefficient use of public funds. Preventing such transfers is, however, difficult, given that one feature of this crisis is the failure of markets to function properly in setting accurate prices. In such a situation, minimizing the scope for unwarranted transfers from the public to the private sector should be one objective of public policy. Similarly, in providing equity injections to banks, it is important that the value of the shares obtained be commensurate with the funds provided. This has not been the case in some countries.

There is a strong presumption that government should set rules to protect taxpayers and to ensure that financial firms play by the rules. These rules entail reorganization when bank capital falls below certain levels. Banks that are too big to fail are not too big to be financially reorganized. Financial reorganizations that shift some of the costs from shareholders and bondholders to taxpayers not only represent an inefficient use of public money but also lead to future moral hazard problems as noted above. Public subsidies to the financial sector lead to distorted resource allocations. The fact that there have been repeated bailouts of the financial sector suggests failures in their ability to assess creditworthiness and systemic problems that must be addressed, both as part of the bailout and of the long-term strategies for preventing future crises. More discussion of these issues is found in Chapter 3.

Six principles should guide bailout design. They should: (a) restore capital adequacy; (b) impose minimal burdens on the public sector budget; (c) establish proper governance/incentive structures; (d) reduce—and certainly not exacerbate—existing problems in the financial system; (e) be viewed as fair to all stakeholders; and (f) be designed to rekindle lending. In some bailout plans, most of the capital has been supplied by the government, while the government has little or no role in management or governance. A failure to align ownership and control almost inevitably gives rise to incentive problems, some of which have been manifest in recent bailouts, where attempts at re-capitalization have been partially undone as the banks have paid out large amounts in bonuses and dividends.

Moreover, some bailouts of financial firms in the wealthiest econo-mies have exacerbated the problems arising from institutions that are "too big to fail." The bailouts have provided money to large failing institutions without penalizing them for their misallocation of re-sources. Moreover, this encourages further consolidation, thereby increasing systemic risk in the future.

Such consolidation strengthens a market structure deeply infused with moral hazard and prone to repeated bouts of excessive risk tak-ing. The mere fact of the vulnerability of the real economy to spill-overs from the financial crisis informs the expectations of risk takers. Confidence in their ability to secure bailouts has been greatest among the very politically influential chief executives of large, highly lever-aged institutions. The international community (through the G-20, Financial Stability Board, and Bank for International Settlements Committees, among others) must give more substantial consideration to the long-term consequences of too-big-to-fail institutions if they are to design sound public policies for the world economy using the les-sons of this crisis. Excessive deference to the wishes of large institu-tions for particular regulatory designs has been, and will continue to be, part of the problem rather than part of the solution to this very damaging experience.

The variety of forms of subsidies to the banking system (including direct subsidies and guarantees) is costly, distorts resource allocations, can distort incentives going forward (the moral hazard problem noted earlier), and creates an unlevel playing field in finance among countries, to the disadvantage especially of those developing countries that cannot afford such subsidies. This is true even if such assistance is viewed to be necessary to stabilize the financial system. Some guarantees may even impede the resolution of bad debts, especially when banking systems allow impaired assets not to be marked to market. Some governments may have undertaken less transparent and less efficient methods of as-sistance to hide the long-run costs from their taxpayers. The potential future costs of all such assistance should be recognized on government budgets at the time the guarantees are provided.

The use of guarantees may also serve to impair the credit quality of the sovereign debt of the country providing the guarantee when the balance sheets of impaired financial institutions are very large in relation to the size of the economy. The credibility and effectiveness of these guarantees may also be called into question in such cases.

Providing more money to financial institutions that supply credit to small and medium-sized enterprises may be viewed as more effective in rekindling lending than giving money to those financial institutions that were more engaged in trading and speculation. In any case, any strategy for restructuring the financial system needs to focus on the functions which the financial system should be providing and take due account of the repeated failures in recent decades.

THE ROLE OF CENTRAL BANKS

Several aspects of the conduct of monetary and credit policies contributed directly to the crisis. The deregulatory pressures of the last two decades as well as the successful management of recent financial crises, which led to a larger appetite for and a lower price of risk, were central to the breakdown of the financial system. Regulators leaning against these currents faced substantial pressure. These issues are discussed more extensively in Chapter 3. This section focuses on central bank monetary policies and the aspects of central bank governance that may affect their conduct of monetary policy. Certain widely held beliefs about the appropriate role for central banks and the appropriate design of their policies may have contributed to these problems.

There has been widespread belief that price stability was necessary and (nearly) sufficient for economic growth and financial stability. However, success in stabilizing goods prices was often accompanied by inflation in asset prices. Decisions to focus on price behavior in the real sector (i.e. on consumer prices) led central banks to ignore the broader impact of financial innovations on risk and liquidity management in financial markets. Thus, while price stability was achieved, central banks did not prevent, and may even have contributed to, the gravest financial turmoil since the Great Depression. In particular, it is clear that the economic cost of this financial fragility was much greater than the economic costs that might have resulted from the slight distortions in resource allocation caused by the relatively modest price misalignments that can arise with uncoordinated price changes in the presence of low to moderate inflation.

Underlying these failures was perhaps an excessive reliance on a particular set of models making unrealistic assumptions concerning rational behavior that ignored key aspects of the economy, including the importance of information asymmetries, the diversity of economic agents, and the behavior of banking institutions. They focused on the efficiencies arising from the diversification of risk associated with securitization while ignoring the problems of information asymmetry to which securitization gave rise.

In the period before the outbreak of the crisis, inflation spread from financial asset prices to petroleum, food, and other commodities, partly as a result of their becoming financial asset classes subject to financial investment and speculation. While it became impossible for central banks to ignore the impact of asset price inflation on goods inflation, the appropriate policy response was not clear. This was the case in particular for central banks following (consumer price) inflation targeting.

Countries that judiciously intervened in their foreign exchange markets and capital markets have fared better than those that did not. Risk absorption mechanisms, especially in developing countries, both in the public and in the private sector are not well developed, and the capacity of firms and households is limited because of low levels of wealth available to absorb shocks of these magnitudes and the lack of development of financial institutions to transfer risks from those less able to bear them to those more able to do so. Those central banks that used the full flexibility implicit in an inflation-targeting approach may also have fared better than those that took a more rigid approach.

One of the lessons of this experience is that monetary policy decisions should be sensitive to the source of inflation. Increasing interest rates to counter the rising prices of tradable goods in an open economy or increasing government-administered prices is unlikely to have much direct impact on inflation. In some developing countries, these sources of inflation can constitute three-fourths or more of GDP. Hence, attempting to rein in inflation by raising interest rates in these cases imposes a high cost on the economy, and especially on interest sensitive non-traded sectors, without providing the desired stabilization of prices.

The recent food and energy crisis also highlighted the problem of the choice of the appropriate target for monetary policy dedicated to price stability. Some central banks have focused on "core inflation," a measure of goods price inflation that excludes the volatile energy and food sectors. But in developing countries this measure of inflation excludes the prices that have the highest impact on household purchasing power and are thus most important in influencing inflationary expectations.

Monetary authorities should, at the same time, be sensitive to the consequences of asset price bubbles and other factors that might affect financial stability and thus economic stability and growth.

Another lesson to emerge from this crisis is that the definitions of national and global macroeconomic stability need to be broadened. It is clear that central banks need to assess the impact of their policies on aspects of stability other than just price stability. In particular, the stability of the real economy and the financial system should also be taken into account. Macroeconomic policy has, of course, broader goals, including growth and employment.

But because these objectives will also be influenced by the behavior of the real economy, including incomes and employment, better coordination of fiscal and monetary policy as well as social policy is required.

While high, accelerating levels of inflation impede expansion and have costs that are inequitably distributed across the population, there is little evidence that moderate, non-accelerating levels of inflation have similar consequences. Moreover, history suggests that deflation represents just as great a threat to economic prosperity as inflation. A gently rising price level can have the merit of speeding up the efficiency of the market process in reallocating resources, especially in the presence of downward wage and price rigidities.

RISKS AND POLICY TRADE-OFFS

Monetary policy has tended to focus exclusively on the stability of prices of real goods and services. Many central bankers claim that asset price stability is either not their responsibility or they do not have the capacity or instruments to control asset prices. Certain central bank governors, for instance, have claimed that they could not ascertain whether there was a speculative element present in market prices or whether there was a bubble, but that even had they been able to do so, they only had one instrument, the interest rate, to deal with two objectives. Using tight interest rates to dampen asset price inflation would have caused an unnecessary sacrifice of real output.

While one cannot ascertain the presence of a speculative bubble with certainty, there are indicators that suggest the likelihood of its presence. But nothing in economics is certain. If policy decisions were restricted to those actions with certain consequences, no decision would ever be taken. Economic policy is always conducted with uncertainty, and part of the art and science of policy making is to assess and balance the risks. It is clear that many central banks erred due to their adherence to erroneous economic creeds which held that misallocation of resources would automatically self-correct with minimal dislocations to the economy.

Multiple Instruments

It is also important to note that central banks do have a number of additional policy instruments at their disposal, such as margin requirements, which—together with other regulatory restrictions discussed in Chapter 3—could have been used to dampen speculative activity in asset markets. It is also not the case that each institution in an economy should use only one instrument and be responsible for only one objective. Such assignments are only viewed as optimal in highly simplified models with little policy value. In a complex economy with considerable interdependence, there are often trade-offs and synergies, requiring multiple instruments to achieve multiple targets. This also needs a high degree of coordination among various institutions.

Changing Structure of the Financial Sector

The large interventions in financial markets by central banks raise a number of other difficult issues, some of which are discussed below. One overriding issue is the effects of large changes in financial markets in recent decades, such as the growth of securitization, the increasing use of leverage, and the decline in the role of relationship banking. Some failings of the financial system may be related to these changes. Another issue is that government intervention will have an effect on the future evolution of the structure of the financial sector. Governments and central banks need to take decisions that they believe will be most effective in generating the benefits that can be derived from a well-performing financial sector—and that will insulate the real economy from the risks to which it has been exposed as a result of the malfunctioning of the financial sector.

Governance

The large role that some central banks have been taking in direct lending to financial institutions raises further questions about the governance of central banks when they are engaged in a quasi-fiscal role. In such a circumstance, is independence from political interference still required by the need to gain "policy credibility?" As already noted, many interventions by central banks have a fiscal character: implicit subsidies and taxes, unfunded or contingent liabilities, etc. While in the past these quasi-fiscal operations were limited and their effect on public finance was more or less regular, they have grown enormously in number and magnitude in the current crisis. The problem is that when central banks engage in quasi-fiscal activity, conventional measures of fiscal activity—such as the deficit of the central government—become misleading indicators of the size or impact of fiscal policy. Therefore, these activities with fiscal implications must be closely coordinated with governments.

MULTIPLE AND NEW OBJECTIVES

Beyond the immediate issues currently being addressed by most countries—stimulating their economies and restarting the flow of credit—there are some basic problems that have to be addressed, such as, in particular, redressing national inequalities and global imbalances. The policies currently being introduced to deal with the economic crisis may exacerbate national inequalities and global imbalances.

The Need for Economic Restructuring

In addition to the problems confronting the global economy described above, many countries face problems in economic restructuring. Rapid increases in productivity in manufacturing, combined with globalization, have translated into rapid improvements in competitiveness in developing countries, which have resulted in rapid changes in comparative advantage across developed and developing countries which in turn have led to changes in the international division of labor. Such adjustments are always very costly and painful, especially when there is high unemployment, where countries provide insufficient adjustment assistance to their citizens or where many citizens have seen large fractions of their wealth, which might have provided a buffer against such changes, disappear. High interest rates and lack of availability of credit—problems facing many developing countries—hinder adjustments and increase the difficulties of economic restructuring. It is important, of course, to avoid the adverse consequences of dysfunctional, under-regulated financial markets, which can lead to overcapacity and fail to allocate capital to high-productivity uses. (Greater availability of capital at low interest rates provides such dysfunctional financial markets greater opportunities to misallocate resources.)

There is also a need to restructure the global economy to meet the challenges of global warming. Providing clear price signals concerning the economic costs associated with global warming would create strong incentives for the private sector, both for households to change consumption patterns and for firms to change production technologies. Restructuring the capital stock would provide large demands for investment that could be a major stimulus for the economy. There may also be a need for government to assist in financing these investments in resource conservation and environmental protection, and so long as markets fail to price these scarce environmental resources appropriately, government subsidies may be required to get efficient resource allocations.

IMPACTS ON DEVELOPING COUNTRIES

Measures are very quickly needed to avoid further deepening of the crisis in emerging markets and other developing countries. These include restoring and expanding social protection and reducing the procyclical features of the economic system. Delay will mean that the eventual cost of dealing with the problem will be higher, and the length and depth of the downturn will be greater, with more innocent victims losing their jobs, with more small, medium and even large businesses forced into bankruptcy.

Why Developing Countries Are Being Hurt So Badly

These ever-present threats have been exacerbated by financial market integration. Many countries have come to rely on foreign banks. Some foreign banks from countries that had inadequate regulation and followed inappropriate macroeconomic policies find their capital badly impaired. They are now repatriating capital with adverse effects on developing countries. The difficulty is compounded by the fact that many developing countries have entered into (North-South) free trade agreements (FTAs), bilateral investment treaties (BITs), and World Trade Organization (WTO) commitments that prevent them from regulating the operations of financial institutions and instruments or capital flows.

For example, if a developing country decides to nationalize some services such as banking, this can require compensation if the sector has been liberalized under the WTO GATS Financial Services Agreements (FSA) or under an FTA or BIT. When these agreements and commitments are enforced, developing countries have to pay compensation or suffer the imposition of tariffs on their exports to the complainant if they do not or cannot comply.

The Role of Protectionism

These adverse effects of financial globalization have been further exacerbated by a new wave of financial protectionism. Governments that have provided large amounts of capital to their banks—either under recapitalization programs or by central banks providing liquidity in unusual ways, with attendant risks to the public finances— understandably expect increased domestic lending. The irony is that this kind of financial protectionism does not seem to be subject to sanctions.

Certain policy measures taken by developed countries have exacerbated these problems further. Credit guarantees have contributed to the reversal of capital flows. Even if developing countries believed it was desirable and appropriate for governments to provide guarantees of the depth and breadth provided by some advanced industrial countries, their guarantees would be less credible. Symmetric policies can have asymmetric effects. Credit guarantees are clearly a violation of the spirit of the "level playing field" in international trade that the international community has attempted to construct over the past half century. Most countries providing such extended guarantees have made no attempt to ensure that those receiving these guarantees pay for them on an actuarially fair basis. In the absence of such full payment, such guarantees represent a major subsidy.

Market forces and resource constraints may also limit the ability of developing countries to pursue counter-cyclical fiscal policies. They may not have sufficient domestic resources, and when they turn to global markets to finance the deficits required to manage counter-cyclical fiscal policies, they may find international markets either unwilling to lend or willing to lend only at very high interest rates. This is one of the reasons that some developing countries have resorted to policies to reduce external constraints and have built up large reserves (see Chapter 5 for a more extensive discussion of these issues).

Market inequities have been exacerbated by government distortions in another way. There have been massive bailouts not only of financial institutions, but also, increasingly, of firms in other sectors of the economy. Most developing countries do not have the resources to match these support measures. Again, this problem may be aggravated if the developing country is party to an international agreement (FTA or BIT). In that case, the agreement would in effect require that if a country wants to support domestic companies facing difficulties, it should provide equal treatment to foreign companies. Here, too, the apparently symmetrical treatment which appears in the agreement can have deeply asymmetrical effects. It would be very difficult for a developing country to bail out a large foreign company, in view of its limited resources, and this could represent an impediment to providing assistance to local companies.

The same consideration applies to public procurement policy. But here again, there is an asymmetry. There are multilateral procurement agreements among developed countries, but relatively few between developed and less-developed countries. Hence, if a developed country adopts a "buy national" policy with an exception for WTO commitments, the effect is to discriminate against purchases from developing countries that do not have such commitments.

In addition, many developing countries have been required by international financial institutions to adopt restrictive policies in times of slow growth or even recession. These policies are markedly different from the counter-cyclical policies adopted by the advanced industrial countries and increase the risks faced by investors in developing countries relative to those in developed countries. In the current crisis, the asymmetry in IMF policy stances has become apparent in several countries. Even the EU is imposing pro-cyclical policies on the enlargement countries, including wage and expenditure reductions in the public sector.

More broadly, developing country dependence on IMF financing has constricted their ability to adopt counter-cyclical policies and other counter-cyclical measures and may impede their willingness to turn to international financial institutions in a timely way, resulting in costly delays.

If strict measures against protectionism are not taken quickly by the international community, developing countries will suffer from the attempts by developed countries to protect themselves from the crisis. In the short and medium term, counter-cyclical policies, social protection measures, infrastructure development, and credit guarantees are indispensable for developing countries and may enhance global fairness.

DEVELOPING COUNTRIES AND FUNDING

Developing countries will need substantial funding in addition to that provided by traditional sources of development assistance to participate effectively in a coordinated global stimulus. They will also need funds to protect their most vulnerable individuals, to provide trade finance and finance to corporations whose sources of international credit may have dried up, and to bolster domestic financial institutions weakened both by the withdrawal of funds and by the precipitous collapse of export earnings. Developing countries also need low-conditionality financing to compensate them for the adverse effects of the intentional and unintentional protectionist measures of the developed countries. (Indeed, additional funding would be required just to offset the imbalances and inequities created by the massive stimulus and bailout measures introduced in the advanced industrial countries.) Current funding available to help developing countries meet the many shocks to which they are regularly exposed, including the volatility in commodity prices, is insufficient.

Sources of funding for developing countries that could be activated quickly and are not subject to inappropriate conditionality are necessary. As in developed countries, substantial portions of this stimulus spending could be directed to environmental measures, especially climate change adaptation, in part fulfilling developed country commitments under the United Nations Framework Convention on Climate Change (UNFCCC).

Failure to maintain the levels of official assistance and to provide this needed additional assistance will have long-term effects. There will be an increase in poverty and malnutrition, and the education of many young people will be interrupted, with lifelong effects. The sense of global social solidarity will be impaired, making agreement on key global issues, such as responding to the challenges of climate change, more difficult. Failure to provide such assistance can even impair the global recovery.

We welcome the decisions of Member States to complete the issuance of Special Drawing Rights (SDRs) approved by the IMF Board in September 1997 through the proposed Fourth Amendment of the Articles of Agreement to double cumulative SDR allocations to SDR 42.8 billion. The issue of additional SDRs could be essential in support of the counter-cyclical financing needs of developing countries. There are a number of possible mechanisms to facilitate the transfer of SDRs to developing countries for this purpose. They are discussed more fully in Chapter 5. Chapter 5 also discusses proposals to provide such emissions on a more regular basis.

In addition, regional efforts to augment liquidity should be supported. For instance, extension of liquidity support under the Chiang Mai initiative without the requirement of an active IMF program should be given immediate consideration. Regional cooperation arrangements can be particularly effective because of a greater recognition of cross-border externalities and greater sensitivities to the distinctive conditions in neighboring countries.

These further sources of funding should be in addition to traditional official development assistance. More broadly, developed countries must make a renewed effort to meet the commitments made in the 2000 Millennium Declaration, the 2002 Monterrey Consensus, the 2005 Global Summit, and the 2008 Doha Declaration.

In thinking about additional funding, it is important to distinguish between support for counter-cyclical macroeconomic policies and longer-term development financing, though increases in the latter can have important counter-cyclical effects. Traditionally, the

World Bank and the regional and sub-regional development banks have played the central role in development lending, while the IMF has played a more important role in managing crises. Some studies have emphasized that the IMF should not play a central role in development assistance. But, what role should it play in the provision of credit in the current crisis, and what role should credit itself play?

Grants and Concessional Lending

At the beginning of the decade, there was considerable concern about the excessive debt burdens of developing countries. In addressing this crisis, it is important to avoid a build-up of unsustainable debt or debt that would crowd out developmental efforts. Thus, the bulk of assistance to the least-developed countries should take the form of transfers rather than loans. There is concern that the initiatives announced by the G-20 in London largely involve additional provision of credit.

A potential source of funding for such assistance would be a commitment by the developed countries to devote 1% of any stimulus package to direct expenditures in developing countries. (There is a similar proposal on the part of the World Bank, which we support.)

The international community should give consideration to accelerated spending accompanied by an early replenishment of International Development Association (IDA) funding. Without an early replenishment, the poorest developing countries may be reluctant to accelerate spending, lest there be inadequate resources available in subsequent years.

The assistance that we call for in this chapter should be viewed as in addition to existing commitments. The advanced industrial countries should fulfill their existing commitments to provide official development assistance.

Social Protection Funds

Over the longer run, the international community should consider establishing a special facility to provide support for those countries creating strong systems of social protection. While such systems may be largely self-funded, it will take time to build up the required reserves, and the international community should consider back-stopping these efforts. Such commitments might have important incentive effects in inducing the creation of such systems, which would also serve to help stabilize the global economic system through their automatic stabilizers.

Comprehensive Involvement

The magnitude of the necessary support could be increased by involving multiple sources of funds, including regional development banks, the IMF, the World Bank, and, possibly, a newly created credit facility to be described below.

Harmonization

While it is essential to continue the important work of harmonization of official development assistance, it is also important that harmonization, especially of counter-cyclical lending, does not lead to concerted imposition of pro-cyclical conditionalities. This is important given the need for countries to quickly undertake measures to stimulate activity, protect the vulnerable, and maintain the flow of credit.

New Credit Facility

The reluctance of many countries to accept assistance from certain institutions and of some potential lenders to provide funds to certain institutions constitutes an impediment that may not be fully addressed by the reforms likely to be made in the short-run. This reluctance may be especially understandable in the light of the current crisis, because some of these institutions pushed policies on to developing countries that are now recognized to have contributed to the crisis and its rapid spread. The availability of alternative mechanisms of disbursement might not only accelerate the flow of funds but also make it less likely that they will be accompanied by pro-cyclical conditionality, either de jure or de facto.

It is thus imperative that during the recovery phase of the crisis, developing countries should have access to additional sources of external funding, including credit and liquidity facilities for social protection, infrastructure investment, and environmental interventions, for government support, for support of developing country financial systems, and for corporate borrowing. Without such support, the global crisis may grow worse, and long-term global cooperation will be impeded.

Existing facilities presently do not meet these needs for several reasons. First, the current system does not provide an efficient mechanism for mobilizing funds available in countries that have accumulated large reserves. It would be beneficial for all participants in the global economy if savings from emerging markets could be utilized in support of developing countries. Government agencies in some emerging market countries that have reserves are reluctant to provide funds to existing multilateral institutions because these countries are underrepresented in their governance structures and the policy advice and conditionalities provided by these institutions are considered inappropriate for the needs of developing countries.

Given the urgent need for rapid response, a new credit facility might be established under the umbrella of existing institutions administered under more representative governance arrangements, or through the creation of new international economic institutions or facilities. Such a new credit facility could draw upon the administrative expertise of existing institutions and could be created rapidly. Its governance would reflect more recent thinking concerning appropriate voice and representation, ensuring greater say not only for those countries providing the funds but also for recipient countries. The governance structure of this facility could be more modular, with regional groupings (for example, the Inter American Development Bank, the Asian Development Bank, the African Development Bank and others) charged with its operations. The introduction of alternative voting arrangements, including double majority voting, should be given serious consideration. Given the limited remit of the IMF's new flexible credit line and the relatively minimal conditionality related to the usage of funds, it may be easier to achieve agreement on the details of governance.

The new funding facilities should be designed with the intention of attracting funds from countries that have accumulated large international non-borrowed reserves. These funding commitments could be backed by guarantees provided by advanced industrial countries. They could be leveraged by borrowing in global financial markets.

With regard to the utilization of the funds, there are different (complementary) options. First, there is an urgent need for balance-of-payment and budget financing, with the objective of increasing developing countries' capacities for counter-cyclical fiscal expenditures. Second, the funds could be used for key investments where some of the emerging markets have a particular interest, such as developing agriculture in African countries, including their capacity to export, thus contributing to food security in other regions, for example in Asian and Arab countries. Another possibility is to use those funds to help developing countries finance guarantees for trade credit or for the debt of their corporations, forestalling the risk of a run on these corporations.

Special consideration should be given to timely environmental investments addressing problems of climate change. The facility could adopt climate change principles to ensure that the short-run focus of this spending is consistent with longer-term development strategies.

CONCLUDING REMARKS

As the world addresses the exigencies posed by this crisis through stimulus packages, monetary and credit policies, and bailouts and guarantees, the international community should not lose sight of remedies for the underlying causes of the crisis and of the other major crises which the world faces—including the food, energy, and climate change crises and the debt crises that have confronted so many poor countries in recent years—nor should it ignore the other major challenges it faces, including the reduction of poverty and inequality. Policies that address the underlying causes are more likely to ensure a robust and quick recovery and to reduce the vulnerability of the global economy to another crisis.

National economic systems which give rise to high levels of inequality pose problems, not only for social and political sustainability but also for economic sustainability, i.e., excessive increases of household and public debt. They may also contribute to an insufficiency of global aggregate demand.

We have noted that responses undertaken by some countries may have exacerbated some of the underlying problems. As noted elsewhere, bank consolidation increases the risk of creating more institutions that are too big to fail, one of the problems contributing to this crisis and making us vulnerable to another. Similarly, poorly designed bailouts may lead to increased inequality. Moreover, unless policies are well designed, there is a risk that national and government debts will be increased unnecessarily, constraining policy space for the future.

The failure of certain national economies to engage in appropriate restructurings and the failure to provide adequate assistance to developing countries without inappropriate conditionalities may contribute to the global imbalances, another major contributing factor to this crisis. Inadequate international responses may (as in the crisis of 1997–1998) contribute to the demand for increased reserves, which in turn may contribute both to global imbalances and to a global insufficiency of aggregate demand.

Of particular concern is that the poorest countries not get themselves into another debt trap, which is why it is of such importance that additional grant funding be provided. In this chapter, we discussed several sources of funding; Chapter 5 discusses several other innovative sources of finance.

Reforms instituted in the last quarter century have put too little emphasis on the properties of an economic system that contributes to *real* stability—properties which reduce its exposure to risk and which enhance its ability to respond to *shocks*. Capital and financial market liberalization has exposed countries to more risk, and, in this crisis, has facilitated the rapid spread of the crisis around the world. We have noted that insufficient attention has been paid to strengthening the built-in stabilizers; in some cases, there have been built-in destabilizers. The next chapter discusses some of the necessary reforms in these areas that can enhance stability. In this chapter, we have noted that there are reforms (like enhanced public and private social insurance systems and more progressive taxation) which simultaneously may address problems of inequality and enhance the stability of the economic system.

It is also of crucial importance that the crisis response should fully take into account the need for transforming the present mode of growth by trying to slow down the overexploitation of natural resources, in particular of those contributing to global warming. This may imply a change in consumer habits to support environmental sustainability. In this respect, investment in new environment and energy technologies, to address adaptation to and mitigation of climate change, is a formidable opportunity for counter-cyclical stimulus. "New environment and energy technologies" (NE^2T) include all technologies able to lower the energy and emissions content of our standard of living, technologies leading to the production of energy from renewable resources, and technologies helping to preserve, repair, and improve ecosystems. For developing countries, the full incremental costs of these investments, justified by their global benefit, should be financed by industrialized countries and transferred to developing countries in exchange for commitments on climate change and biodiversity. Such resource commitments have already been made as part of earlier international environmental conventions, but substantial additional resources to fulfill those commitments have yet to be provided. The imperative to address this question is enhanced by the fact that while developed countries are, by far, the biggest global polluters up to now, some emerging market economies could soon become the biggest global polluters. It is thus rational to make large investments today to develop those technologies and to make them available freely to developing and emerging countries through technological transfer. Climate change and biodiversity are quintessential global public goods. Supporting developing countries in their own efforts to address climate change and preserve biodiversity should be seen as part of the solution, and of the way the international community can ensure that these global objectives are effectively addressed.

More generally, the need to retrofit the global economy for the exigencies of global warming can provide an important source of aggregate demand (if accompanied by appropriate regulatory policies and policies on the pricing of carbon and if accompanied by adequate finance) to help pull the economy out of the current global economic downturn.

To date, there has been little effort to coordinate international responses to the crisis. Reactions in almost all countries have been simply to launch national recovery programs. These programs have been nationally designed with almost no coordination among countries, even in the Euro area. Traditional thinking, derived from crises arising in a single country, entails identifying areas in which domestic multipliers are high. But that kind of approach may lead to recovery programs that are far from optimal not only in magnitude but in design, delivering less global stimulus relative to the size of the increase in total spending or indebtedness. Moreover, underlying problems, like global imbalances, may not only not be addressed but may also be exacerbated. There is a special need for surplus countries to take strong actions. Moreover, macroeconomic coordination would avoid the risk of self-defeating beggar-thy-neighbor strategies aimed at increasing exports while attempting to decrease imports, or increasing credit available to home country firms at the expense of credit available elsewhere. These new forms of protectionism can be as detrimental to the global economic system as the old and more unfair to developing countries. Protectionism through subsidies and guarantees are particularly disturbing, since developing countries cannot match the subsidies and guarantees given by developed countries.

Because countries are at different phases of their business cycles, and different countries have different automatic stabilizers and destabilizers, mechanisms for coordinating macroeconomic policy and evaluating relative contributions will be difficult. Moreover, different countries have different circumstances—for instance, different inherited debt burdens—suggesting different capacities to implement counter-cyclical policies. Developing countries, in particular, have greater external dependence and vulnerability to external cycles and much weaker capacity to undertake counter-cyclical policies.

Still, if governments bear in mind that what is important is not just their liabilities (the national debt) but their national balance sheet (their assets as well), and if they direct much of the stimulus to investments (in infrastructure, technology, and human capital), then the stimulus spending can leave the country in a stronger position and can be sustained for a longer period of time. This is especially important given that this crisis may be an extended one.

A cross-cutting issue is the need for significant improvements in regulatory cooperation. Regulatory and tax arbitrage distort capital allocation and undermine government efforts at reinvigorating their economies that have been the subject of this chapter. This is the subject of the next.

3

REFORMING GLOBAL REGULATION TO ENHANCE GLOBAL ECONOMIC STABILITY

INTRODUCTION: THE ECONOMIC CRISIS AND THE FAILURE OF FINANCIAL MARKET REGULATION

This global economic recession is the worst since the Great Depression. It originated in the financial sector in the United States and some other advanced industrial countries. The financial sector is supposed to manage risk, allocate capital, and mobilize savings, all at the lowest possible transaction costs. In many countries, including the U.S., the financial system failed to perform these vital functions and yet absorbed large amounts of society's resources, including some of its more capable individuals. Mistakes in the financial sector have imposed large costs on taxpayers. This is not the first time that the failure of financial markets to perform these essential functions has led to severe losses of wealth and an economic recession. Indeed, financial crises and bailouts are a regular feature of the market economy.

Furthermore, in recent years, the size and scale of financial market activity in relation to the underlying economy has led some to question whether unfettered free markets had promoted finance, the servant, to the position of master of the economy and, more broadly, society. As noted earlier, in many countries financial markets had become ends in themselves rather than a means to a more productive economy. The measure of success of financial policy should not be the rate of growth or the size of the financial sector as a share of GDP. Indeed, an excessively large financial sector relative to the GDP of a medium to large economy should be a cause of concern to those interested in long-term economic growth because financial crises are often associated with unsustainable growth of the financial sector.

Since capital is more scarce in developing countries, mistakes in risk management and capital allocation impose heavier burdens on them. The large diversion of some of their most talented individuals to finance is also particularly costly. So too are the consequences of a failure of their financial systems to mobilize savings and the unnecessarily large transactions costs, including an inefficient and costly payments mechanism.

As noted above, these failures have been particularly costly for developing countries. Without foreign assistance they may not be able to implement the stimulus packages necessary for recovery. This crisis will leave a heavy legacy of debt on even the wealthiest of countries, including the United States, but for many already overly indebted developing countries, the burdens of rescuing the financial sector failure can be even greater. Resources committed to recapitalize financial institutions might have been better spent in promoting growth, including investments in education, health, infrastructure, and technology.

Even in countries that were desperately in need of mobilizing savings, financial markets encouraged consumption. Had the financial sector in richer countries, such as the U.S., performed their critical function of allocating the ample supply of low cost funds to productive uses, the world economy might now be facing a boom rather than today's economic crisis.

While in many countries financial markets did not perform the roles that they should have and diverted scarce resources from other sectors where they might have been more socially productive, there have been other adverse social consequences. Compensation schemes in financial markets resulted in huge societal inequalities, and the economic disruptions to which dysfunctional financial markets gave rise imposed special burdens on the poor and less-well-educated.

There is an extensive literature explaining the reasons for the pervasive and persistent failure of financial institutions. In spite of the widespread presumption in favor of private markets, research over the last three decades has shown that they do not in general produce efficient outcomes when information is imperfect and especially when information asymmetries mean that different individuals will have different information. Such information imperfections are particularly pervasive in financial markets. Moreover, in financial markets, private incentives, both at the level of the organization and the individual decision-maker, are often not aligned with social returns. While this crisis has made evident that there are large disparities in all countries, they may be of particular significance in developing economies.

Because of the pervasive and persistent "failure" of financial institutions to perform their essential roles, they are regulated by governments. The quarter century following World War II is noteworthy for its absence of financial crises, and this is almost surely the result of the more stringent regulatory regime of the New Deal and similar regulations in the rest of the world that were imposed in the aftermath of the Great Depression.

However, the current crisis comes on the heels of a period of time when many political leaders and economists espoused deregulation. They argued either that the inherent efficiency of unfettered financial markets would contribute to the overall efficiency of the economy or at least that "lighter" regulation would improve economic performance. These claims put little emphasis on the notion of market imperfections and externalities. While earlier economic episodes as well as modern economic theory should have led to skepticism, the sheer magnitude and pervasiveness of this crisis is a profound refutation of that vision (which is sometimes referred to as free-market fundamentalism or neoliberalism).

There is now a consensus that inadequate regulations and regulatory institutions, some of which failed even to implement effectively those regulations that existed, contributed to this crisis. While "blame" should rest on the financial sector, government failed to protect the market from itself and to protect society from the kinds of excesses that have repeatedly imposed high costs on taxpayers, workers, home owners, and retirees.

Regulation, Rationality, and Self-Regulation

The doctrines that supported deregulation were predicated on the assumption that sophisticated market participants were rational and had rational expectations. They were considered to view market prices as the best available signals for the allocation of resources. Indeed, the standard view went even further and argued that unfettered markets would result in optimum economic efficiency. Under these assumptions only self-regulation was appropriate. The only role for government regulation was protection for small investors who might not be fully informed. Rationality was presumed to result from the fact that those who were "irrational" would suffer losses and thus be excluded from the market through bankruptcy.

But this standard view ignored key advances in economics in the last quarter century—and especially results relating to the inefficiency of markets when it is recognized that information is always imperfect and asymmetric. Such informational asymmetries are also an inherent characteristic of financial markets. Theoretical arguments have been bolstered by a wealth of historical experience and econometric evidence suggesting: (a) that markets are generally not self-correcting; (b) that financial markets in particular are usually characterized by "market failures;" and (c) that failures in financial markets have systemic consequences for the economy.

The assumption of rationality is thus even more questionable in financial markets. There is, indeed, a long historical experience of crises in financial markets, with dire consequences for output and employment. The large externalities associated with failure of financial institutions means that other institutions may be affected by this process. That is why banks that have failed in their minimal task of credit assessment have been repeatedly rescued. But even if all market participants are rational and there is no systemically significant financial institution, regulation is necessary because of external effects arising out of correlated behavior. Put simply, the traditional (pre-crisis) remit of financial regulation was just too narrow.

To a large extent, the views of those political leaders that espoused deregulation were supported by economic models based on these flawed ideas. The models used to describe the economic process and the underlying (often implicit) assumptions have, of course, long been the subject of controversy. This extraordinarily costly crisis provides an opportune time to reopen these debates and to learn from recent experience about market and political processes as well as the desirable regulatory regime. In particular, views about the efficiency (or failures) of market processes will affect views about the appropriate regulatory regime—as will perspectives about the capacity of governments to correct market failures.

The recent experience should not only greatly invigorate debate but also lend support to those who questioned the models of competition and efficient markets with well-informed individuals and firms (typically with rational expectations) that justified the deregulatory policies.

The Resurgence of an Understanding of the Need for Regulation

The current crisis may thus be considered a direct consequence of these ideas which supported the elimination of many regulations that had enhanced the ability of markets to function efficiently. Some of the regulations had been adopted in the aftermath of the Great Depression. They should have been adapted to the evolving markets, not eliminated. Moreover, the changing economy—the creation of new financial instruments—required new regulations. Even when adequate regulations were in place, many regulators didn't believe in the need for regulation and, not surprisingly, did not enforce it effectively. The crisis highlights the imperative for regulations and a regulatory structure reflecting the changing economy and strengthened supervision of the entire financial system.

As the Congressional Oversight Panel of the financial bailout package (the TARP) in the United States concludes in its report on regulatory reform: "But at the root, the regulatory failure that gave rise to the current crisis was one of philosophy more than structure."[1] Had there been a greater appreciation of the role of regulation, the United States could have implemented an effective set of regulations within existing regulatory institutions. Still, reforms in regulatory institutions may be called for to prevent the capture of the regulatory process by those whose interests (and philosophy) argue against the need for strong regulation.

To illustrate, at a very simple level, why regulation is necessary, consider a situation where the failure of a large, complex financial institution can do great harm to the economy and in which policy makers will act to mitigate the consequences for the real economy—a bailout. It is easy to see that, without adequate regulation, private incentives to take risk are not those that are socially optimal. Ex ante, there are two possibilities (regulation, no regulation) and ex post two possibilities (bailout, no bailout).

	Bailout	No Bailout
Regulation	A	B
No Regulation	C	D

A *true* adherent of a free market would seek to impose a regime of no regulation and no bailouts—position D in the matrix. Let us assume for the purpose of the argument that the social payoff that would result from the choice of D might be larger than in any of the other regimes, even though in reality it may not be. D represents an optimal system design as long as no financial institution is large enough that its failure would impose sufficient harm to the real economy to induce the authorities to break the pledge of no bailouts. In fact, in all countries there are sufficiently large financial institutions that the entire right column is simply not credible since there is no way that the government can commit itself not to bail out a big bank. Thus, the real choice for society is between positions A and C. The management of large financial institutions knows this ex ante. Given that in the future any financial crisis will elicit a bailout, only the imposition of regulations (Regime A) can restrain financial institutions from exploiting the misalignment of social and private incentives. In Regime B, banks would undertake *excessive risk* given their belief that the position of no bailout is not sustainable and that any losses will be covered by a government bailout. This simple logic has become powerfully obvious in the recent crisis. To repeat, given that governments cannot commit themselves not to bail out large banks, economic efficiency requires that they be regulated and that position A is the only viable solution.

This example illustrates a situation where the private incentives of the financial institution do not coincide with those of society more generally. Such a situation can arise even when no single financial institution is too large to fail. If a number of smaller institutions exhibit correlated behavior, their actions can give rise to a systemic problem requiring a government bailout, and again, their incentives will not be appropriately aligned with those of society.

In fact, the current crisis opens up debates not only on how to use regulatory policy to align private and social incentives for firms but also how to align managerial incentives within the large financial institutions to reduce the incentives for decision-makers within those firms to take risks that are borne by the firm as a whole, the owners of the resources they manage, and society at large.

These problems are referred to in the economics literature as "agency" issues because they deal with the difficulties that arise when agents have objectives that differ from those of the individuals *on whose behalf* they are empowered to act. For example, the savings of workers held in pension funds is invested by portfolio managers who act as agents. But the welfare of the managers may not be perfectly aligned with those of the workers. Indeed, managers seldom attempt to induce the firms to act in ways that are consonant with the interests of the worker; more frequently, they focus on very short-term returns.

Thus, modern economies are marked by a long chain of agency problems: the 19th century model of capitalism, in which the owner managed his own firm, is increasingly rare, particularly in advanced industrial societies. While perfect alignment of interests is impossible, the current crisis has illustrated the magnitude of their disparity and heightened the need for regulations which bring them more closely in alignment.

Regulatory Structures and Institutions

While there is a clear case for government regulation of financial markets, governments often fail to adopt the appropriate regulatory structures. The incentives faced by public officials, regulators, and elected officials, and the role of money in politics are important antidotes to romantic notions of the efficacy of regulation to correct for market failures.

Even when appropriate regulations are adopted, they may not be effectively enforced. Regulators may be 'captured' by those that they are supposed to regulate. Even expertise can be captured, as experts are themselves motivated by considerations of power, prestigious awards, and compensation. The design of regulatory institutions should take into account these risks.

Before the crisis there was a heated debate between those who favored regulation based on "principle" and based on "rules." The former were concerned that banks would use rules as goalposts that would allow them to circumvent basic banking principles, while the latter were concerned about the possibility of regulatory capture. But the crisis overwhelmed both rule-based and principle-based regulatory systems, suggesting that this dichotomy was not as important as it may have appeared. Both principles that set out the objectives of regulation and rules that try to apply these principles appear to be required.

While ideas matter, so do interests: the current regulatory regime may have been affected more by the influence of certain special interests than the merits of theoretical arguments. These special interests may, in particular, have found those ideas that supported their positions particularly appealing and did what they could to promote them.

Ensuring global financial stability to support economic stability is a global public good. In a world of financial and economic integration, a failure in the financial system of one large country (or even a moderately sized one) can exert large negative externalities on others. This was brought home in the 1997–1998 global financial crisis as fears of "contagion" became widespread. Such contagion was, indeed, evident as the crisis in East Asia led to problems in Russia, and the crisis in Russia spread in turn to Brazil. But the present crisis has made these "cross-border spillovers" particularly evident, as the failure of the U.S. to regulate its financial markets adequately has had global consequences. That is why a discussion of regulation is not just a matter that can or should be left to national authorities. There has to be global coordination. It is also why the subject is one of the principle concerns of this report.

This chapter sets forth some general principles of financial sector regulation and some reforms needed to bring existing national and international regulatory practices in line with these principles. It makes certain key distinctions between micro-regulation aimed at the behavior of particular financial institutions and macroeconomic regulations directed at the systemic stability of the financial system and enhancing macroeconomic stability. While the general principles of regulation and the purpose and functions of particular aspects of regulation need to be specified, the particular institutional framework and implementation of these regulations should be tailored to the circumstances of each domain.

This chapter also lays out key issues in the design of *financial policy*—that is, government interventions in the financial sector. Most of the discussion focuses on regulation, but financial policy goes beyond regulation. It may include creating incentives for the provision of credit to certain underserved groups or creating institutions that focus on long-term development impacts rather than the short-term capital gains that have been the central focus of so much of the financial market. It includes providing incentives for catalyzing the creation of financial institutions or instruments that help meet social needs—mortgages that help individuals manage the risks of home ownership better, student loans with lower transaction costs, banking the un-banked, or insuring the uninsured. In short, it entails all interventions other than the attempt by government to make *private* financial institutions behave better, that is, more in accord with general principles of efficiency, for instance, by better alignment of social and private benefits.

Therefore, banking regulation needs to be seen as part of financial market regulation, and financial market regulation needs to be seen more broadly as part of overall financial policy. There are several important forms of financial market regulation: (i) protecting consumers and investors (rules against fraud, market manipulation, misrepresentation of products, and laws promoting competition); (ii) ensuring the safety and soundness of individual institutions; (iii) ensuring competition; (iv) ensuring systemic stability; (v) promoting deep financial development, particularly long-term finance; and (vi) ensuring access to finance. Ensuring systemic stability goes beyond ensuring the safety and soundness of individual institutions. Such regulations can support and safeguard confidence in the financial system as a whole and enhance financial and economic stability. While they may not be able to prevent crises such as the current one, they can make them less frequent and less severe. Promoting macroeconomic stability goes beyond avoiding crises; it entails the expansion of credit when the economy is in a downturn and the curtailment of credit when inflation threatens.

Similarly, financial market regulation has multiple objectives: (i) promoting financial market stability; (ii) enhancing macroeconomic stability and growth; (iii) promoting the efficiency of the allocation of scarce capital; (iv) promoting equity; and (v) protecting the public finances which have borne the financial consequences of regulatory failures.

Governments need to be aware of the relationships among the various forms of regulation and regulatory institutions and the relationship between regulations and other instruments of government policy, all of which are aimed at ensuring that financial markets perform their vital role in support of all members of society.

Many areas of government policy such as competition policy and corporate governance are as relevant to the financial sector as they are to other sectors. Indeed, some of the worst failures of the financial system may be traced to failures in these two areas.

There may be trade-offs: a less competitive financial system may be more stable but less efficient and give rise to greater social inequities. But there are also important complementarities. The financial system's failure is in part a result of predatory lending; better and better enforcement of investor protection would have resulted in a more stable financial system.

But regulations are not costless. As always, there must be balance between costs and benefits. Today, the global economy is paying a very high price for inadequate and inappropriate regulations as well as a failure to effectively enforce those that did exist. Clearly, regulators in the main financial centers of the world failed to get the balance right, and their failures have imposed heavy costs on the global economy. The additional costs of better regulation are dwarfed by the costs imposed on society by the failure to regulate.

One of the often-alleged costs of tighter regulation is that it might slow the pace of innovation. There is little evidence that the innovations in the financial sector in recent years have enhanced the overall performance of the economy, though to be sure it may have increased the profits of the sector. Much of the innovative effort of the sector was directed at circumventing regulations, taxes, and accounting standards; other innovations increased revenues generated through higher transactions costs. These "innovations" had a negative social return.

Only a small fraction of the U.S. financial sector, the venture capital firms, was directed at promoting innovation in the productive sector. This part of the financial sector is now under strain. More generally, there is a risk that financial markets will emerge from the crisis with a financial system that is less well equipped to meet the future needs of our society. It may, for instance, be less competitive. The need for appropriate regulations may be even greater now than it was in the past.

The rest of this chapter discusses at greater length some of the general principles of financial market regulation. It first focuses on transparency and incentives and macro- and micro-regulation, respectively. It then discusses financial market restructuring and regulatory institutions. While most of the issues discussed to this point relate to national financial systems, the chapter then examines global regulation and the problems that are posed by cross-border capital flows. It concludes with the presentation of a broader range of issues in financial policy that go beyond regulation.

THE PURPOSES AND GENERAL PRINCIPLES OF FINANCIAL REGULATION

Firms operating in the financial sector are regulated over and above other firms for two principal reasons. This section reviews the justifications for regulation and the possible types of regulation appropriate to these institutions.

Consumer and Investor Protection

The first reason is that consumers of financial products require additional protection from those provided for other products because their performance cannot easily be tested before, at, or shortly after the point of purchase. As already noted, monitoring banks and their ability to fulfill their contractual promises is a public good. The present crisis has highlighted, in addition, the need to protect many individuals from predatory lending practices, where financial institutions took advantage of those who were ill equipped to make judgments concerning the risks associated with the financial products that were sold. But even relatively well-informed individuals cannot assess the riskiness of the complex financial products being sold or the appropriateness of these products to their circumstances. Issues of consumer and investor protection are discussed at greater length later in this chapter.

EXTERNALITIES AND REGULATION

The second reason is that financial markets are particularly prone to exhibit externalities. This crisis has shown how the failures of the financial system have imposed costs on others, such as taxpayers, home owners, and workers, who were not directly party to the excessive risk-taking. Indeed, the failures affected the world economy at large, plunging the world into its worst peacetime recession since the 1930s. Whenever there are externalities, there is a divergence between private incentives and social returns, and the magnitude of the disparity in this present case clearly calls for strong government action.

Financial markets are characterized by imperfect information, and as already noted, markets with imperfect information are often characterized by serious inefficiencies requiring government intervention. Such information imperfections give rise to significant externalities and externality-like effects.

The Special Role of Banks

The role that banks (institutions licensed and regulated for deposit taking and other banking operations with access to liquidity from central banks) play in a credit economy is unique and quite different from the role played by non-banks such as traditional investment bank broker-dealers, mutual funds, insurance companies, and hedge funds. The crisis has also highlighted that bank access to central bank liquidity and provision of liquidity to the rest of the economy played a critical role in the transmission of the boom.

The distinctive role of banks is in part related to their role in the payments mechanism. This distinction provides a basis for recommendations to regulate the activities of core banking activities (deposits from individuals and loans to companies) more heavily than non-bank institutions, while making regulation more comprehensive across the national and international financial system.

The distinctive role of banks was obscured in the run-up to this crisis. Some financial institutions engaged in the creation of arms-length off-balance-sheet entities, such as special investment vehicles, that engaged in banking-like activities without being subject to regulation or access to central bank support or deposit insurance. This "shadow banking system" took on an increasingly important role in providing credit, and some aspects of the credit crunch were related to failures in these shadow banks.

In addition, the banking system became intertwined with other financial institutions in ways that meant that the failure of these other financial institutions (AIG) could put the banking system at risk.

The failure to effectively regulate these interlinkages as well as other aspects of the risk position of banks has resulted in taxpayers becoming unintended bearers of the residual risk of a failure of the financial institutions that had provided explicit or implicit guarantees to the shadow banking system. Not only does this result in excessive risk taking, but it also distorts the financial market structure, since there are large implicit subsidies associated with such guarantees.

Externalities and the Failure of Self-Regulation

Because of the externalities that play such a large role in motivating regulation, it should have been clear that the self-regulation that was promoted so forcefully in the deregulation movement that preceded the crisis made little sense. Self-regulation in the presence of externalities is an oxymoron.

Network Linkages and Externalities

The nature of the credit economy is such that the lending by one bank often serves as a deposit at another, and this deposit may be used to provide collateral for borrowing at a third. An essential part of banking is that banks lend to banks, and so a failure of one can lead to a cascade of failures. This means that the behavior of individual banking institutions can have systemic influence in a way that a failure of, say, a shoe shop may not. The failure of a single bank can bring down the entire financial system, either directly or as a result of a general loss of confidence in all banks, leading to a freeze in inter-bank markets. At other times, this discussion might appear merely academic, but the credit crunch has underscored the systemic nature of bank failures and the role of confidence and trust.

The Key Role of Trust and Confidence and the Role of Regulation

Confidence and trust is essential because an individual turns over his capital to a financial institution with the promise that he will get it back, with an expected return, at a later date. But these promises are often broken. Moreover, it is costly for individuals to ascertain whether a particular bank will be able to fulfill this promise. The complexity of modern finance has made this increasingly difficult, but many financial institutions in the run-up to this crisis deliberately tried to obfuscate their financial position (both from regulators and investors). When those who have entrusted their money to a particular financial institution lose confidence, they will pull their money out, and the financial institution may collapse. Many financial institutions have given good reason that they should not be trusted.

Government regulation can play a key role in the restoration and maintenance of trust and confidence in financial institutions. Some one hundred years ago, Americans lost trust in the safety of their meat packing industry; trust was only restored with government regulation. The failure of self-regulation and the rating agencies provides further bases for a strong role of government regulation in current circumstances.

Regulation and Monitoring: Information As a Public Good

Moreover, information is a public good. There is no marginal cost of an additional individual using a particular piece of information, including information about the creditworthiness of a bank. When public goods are privately provided, there will typically be an undersupply and/or large inefficiencies, as barriers are created to the enjoyment of something for which the marginal cost is low (zero). This provides another rationale for public monitoring of financial institutions.

Moreover, most individuals lack the technical competence to evaluate the financial position of a bank. Indeed, even the regulators and the rating agencies, which were presumed to have specialized competence, failed to do a good job. These problems are compounded by failures in the "rating agency market," described more extensively below, making reliance on such private assessments problematic at best.

TRANSPARENCY AND INCENTIVES

While all regulation is designed to induce private firms to alter their behavior to bring it more into line with the interests of society as a whole, it is often difficult for government (regulators) to control behavior directly or even to ascertain what appropriate behavior entails. For instance, while everyone agrees that banks should not engage in excessively risky behavior, what does that entail? Modern regulation is predicated on a multi-pronged approach that includes direct restrictions on behavior as well as restrictions affecting the determinants of behavior. The most important determinants are incentives and competition. If markets are to exercise discipline, they must have access to good information, which implies transparency, and there must be effective competition. There were significant deficiencies in both competition and transparency in the run-up to this crisis (and these conditions still prevail).

Transparency

Good information is required for the efficient functioning of the market economy. Part of the failure of this crisis is a failure of information.

The financial sector demonstrated its ability to use creative accounting to obscure information. If market participants do not know the risks undertaken by banks or other publicly listed companies, it is difficult to assess appropriately the value of shares and bonds. This means that capital may not be allocated efficiently. Transparency is important for markets to exercise discipline by producing efficient prices. How can the decision to buy or sell a bank's shares and bonds be determined accurately if the risks to which it is exposed are not known? Regulatory reforms must deal adequately with these issues of transparency.

But while stronger transparency is necessary for a better functioning financial system, this is not enough. It is unlikely that, in aggregate, the excessive lending and borrowing that helped fuel the present crisis would have been substantially reduced if there had been greater transparency. Nor would full disclosure make the accurate appraisal of the risks of very complex financial products possible. The lack of transparency is often a symptom of deeper market failures that produces incentives to limit information, and these deeper market failures may have other manifestations. Moreover, lack of transparency is only one of several market failures.

There is now widespread agreement that private markets do not necessarily provide optimal incentives for transparency. There may even be incentives for providing distorted information, e.g., incentives associated with executive compensation schemes based on stock options. Regulatory arbitrage also provides incentives to reduce transparency. The creation of off–balance sheet vehicles that caused so much difficulty in the current crisis was the result of such arbitrage. Regulations should not only ensure greater transparency, they should also improve incentives for transparency. Thus, requirements for expensing of stock options or increasing capital adequacy requirements for those banks that pay executives through stock options reduce the incentives to use them.

Mark-to-market accounting was introduced to increase transparency. But some have argued that its inappropriate application to all assets contributes to market volatility. The problem is not with mark-to-market accounting but with how the information provided is used by firms, markets, and regulators. The adverse effects of mark-to-market accounting could be offset by countercyclical capital adequacy requirements and provisioning described below. It would be a major retreat from transparency to move away from mark-to-market accounting.

However, the regulatory system should reward financial institutions with long-term funding of liabilities. In this regard, mark-to-funding could be more useful than mark-to-market accounting and in some cases even more relevant. Life insurance firms, for instance, with long-term liabilities but with assets matching those liabilities should not be placed at a disadvantage. But this is what would happen with mark-to-market accounting if liquidity risk spreads rose and the long-term assets in which they had invested fell in value. It would be inefficient to match each asset with its funding, but pools of assets could be matched with pools of funding. One difficulty in a mark-to-funding approach would be determining the maturity of funding. Life insurance policies might normally be held to maturity, but the contract provides a liquidity option—owners can borrow against them. They also have a cash value. Demand deposits are normally held for a long time, but in a panic, they can be withdrawn overnight.

Accounting standards should make information as transparent as possible for shareholders and bondholders. This might require changing existing standards. For example, while dynamic, counter-cyclical provisioning is desirable, accounting standards boards are not currently well disposed to such proposals. They prefer event-based to statistical accounting, even though statistical techniques may be the best means for providing reliable estimates of future losses.

While mark-to-market value accounting may not be appropriate for the risk management of some institutions, it is important to recognize that failure to apply it may induce other perverse incentives, particularly during crises. Banks may have an incentive to engage in excessive risk taking—assets that go down in price may be kept while those that go up in price may be sold. The result is to increase the divergence between market values and "book" values. This incentive has been compounded by recent actions to, in effect, suspend mark-to-market accounting in the crash, having promoted it in the boom.

Transparency regulations have to be comprehensive. Otherwise there is a risk that transactions which market participants do not want to disclose fully will be channeled through the less transparent vehicle. As noted below, this is a concern with recent proposals that do not require full transparency in over-the-counter trading in derivatives such as credit default swaps. Giving banks and firms a choice of using either not-fully-disclosed over-the-counter stock options or fully disclosed exchange-traded options might encourage less transparency. (Regulation of derivatives is discussed more fully below.)

Moreover, without such comprehensiveness, it will be difficult for those who wish to use the information to assess its relevance. In the global financial crisis of 1997–1998, many developing countries argued that without transparency requirements imposed on hedge funds' holdings of their liabilities, it would be difficult for them to ascertain their risk exposure. While other market participants might make full disclosure, it would be difficult for these countries, or other market participants, to ascertain the adequacy of their foreign exchange reserves without full and comprehensive disclosure.

Regulations should also be directed at affecting incentives for transparency (or lack of transparency). Compensation systems relying heavily on stock market performance provide strong incentives for the provision of distorted information. This provides a further argument for restricting the form of compensation (in addition to those discussed more extensively below). More generally, there are managerial incentives to reducing transparency, especially in economies with inadequate corporate governance. Reduced transparency may reduce the threat of a takeover and may enhance the ability of executives to enhance their compensation.

Economic theory suggests that transparency may actually lead to more volatility. But even if this proves to be the case, most of the time the benefits of transparency outweigh the costs, and so there should be a strong presumption for greater transparency. Without good information, resources cannot be efficiently allocated, and lack of transparency can too easily contribute to exploitation and corruption.

Just as accounting standards should allow for as much information and transparency as possible, the same should be the case for the promulgation and implementation of regulations. While supervisors are, in principle, free to ask for information from private actors, the public dissemination of any findings needs to be carefully handled. The supervisor should have an obligation to put transactions involving public money in the public domain but perhaps with a lag, if there are concerns about market sensitivity. If proprietary information issues restrict full disclosure of firm-level data, there should be full disclosure of aggregate data.

Transparency should be encouraged whenever a financial rescue plan is being undertaken. In the current scenario, the manner in which financial rescues/bailouts are being conducted is often opaque and uncertain. As a result, a great deal of confusion has been sown about the principles underlying the financial restructuring that is occurring and about the process by which the terms are determined. This has contributed to market uncertainty. While in the past, a simple adage—"save the banks, not the bankers"—has been followed, in the current crisis this important distinction has been blurred in some countries. Clear principles need to be in place that recognize that, while banks may be systematically important, this is not the case for all elements of their capital structures. An expedient resolution—through recapitalization, (temporary) nationalization, and/or super (or expedited) "Chapter 11" bankruptcy (conservatorship)—could restore the credit intermediation process in the most rapid and transparent manner possible.

Incentives

Incentives are thus key to an efficient and effective operation of the financial system. Regulators need to make sure that the incentives of financial institutions and those of management are compatible with the social objectives of the financial system. It will never be possible to monitor and regulate all the practices that expose banks and the economy to excessive risk. It is therefore imperative to get incentives right. It is clear that private rewards have not been linked to social returns. This means that there are perverse incentives that produce adverse outcomes.

The fact that so many firms have adopted incentive structures that served shareholders and other stakeholders well in the short-run but so poorly in the long-run is suggestive of serious and pervasive failures in corporate governance. Weaknesses in corporate governance in both developed and developing countries have long been recognized, but not enough has been done. While such problems exist in all sectors, they may have more dire consequences in the financial sector. This crisis should provide an opportunity to revisit these issues.

The payment of large bonuses to top executives of banks that have had record losses shows that "incentive pay" was not closely related to performance—something that statistical studies have also confirmed. One long-recognized problem is that current incentive structures encourage excessive risk-taking and short-sighted behavior. Not only did such incentive structures play an important role in the run-up to the crisis, but they have also impeded attempts to resolve it. Methods to remedy these problems include requiring incentive compensation schemes to be based on long-term performance and implementation of a requirement that firms pay higher capital charges if their remuneration schemes are not designed to limit excessive risk-taking. Stock options should be reported as a form of remuneration—expensed and valued at the time of issue or of resetting stock option strike prices. In any case, payment through stock options can provide particularly perverse incentives because it encourages deceptive accounting practices that contribute to (temporarily) high stock prices. Using indicators other than the performance of share prices could create incentive schemes more commensurate with social objectives, e.g., by rewarding achievements in corporate social responsibility.

When banks become too big to fail, they have perverse incentives for excessive risk-taking. Problems are even worse if a financial institution is judged to be too big to be financially resolved (at least in times of a crisis). It is imperative that governments impose strong antitrust policies with criteria stronger than just market power. (See the discussion below.)

Regulators should be particularly attentive to conflicts of interest. For instance, investment bank analysts' views affect markets, and those views may be influenced by the positions they hold. There can also be conflicts of interest between the roles of financial institutions as commercial banks and as investment banks. Similarly, credit rating agencies were paid by those whose creditworthiness they were supposed to evaluate. Disclosure is an important first step.

The privately owned, government-sponsored enterprise (GSE), such as Fannie Mae and Freddie Mac, in which the government either provides conditional funding or guarantees to a firm with private shareholders and independent management given wide latitude, may be a particularly hard model to design in a way that avoids potential conflicts between managerial interests in maximizing their own returns, returns to shareholders, and the overall public interest.

REGULATION AND INNOVATION

One alleged potential cost of regulation is to reduce the scope and speed of financial innovation. But much of the recent innovation in the financial system has sought to increase the short-run profitability of the financial sector rather than to increase the ability of financial markets to better perform their essential functions of managing risk and allocating capital. In addition, innovation has engendered financial instability. Indeed, from the point of view of the economy as a whole, some innovations had a clearly negative impact. It is important to design regulatory structures that encourage economic and socially productive innovations and to place adequate constraints on socially dubious innovation; good regulation may actually enhance the scope for positive innovation.

In some cases, a slight delay in introducing an innovation in order to ascertain better whether it makes a positive or negative contribution to the economy or to determine its suitability for particular purposes would have little cost but would produce substantial benefits by ensuring that inappropriate products are not marketed or sold to those for whom they are inappropriate.

In fact, just as financial market failures noted above led to excessive risk taking, short-sighted behavior, and exploitation of financially unsophisticated individuals, it also led to "innovations" that were not necessarily welfare enhancing from the perspective of society. At the same time, few incentives were provided for innovations that would have been welfare enhancing.

An outsized financial sector, often acting non-competitively, impeded innovations such as an efficient electronic payment system based on modern communications technology. Innovations that would have led to more stable mortgage markets or other innovations that would have enabled households and countries to manage the critical risks they face, including the risks associated with home ownership, were not introduced because they challenged the vested interests of large institutions. The failure to produce mortgages that enabled even average Americans to manage the risk of home ownership better is now having disastrous global consequences.

The financial sector also failed to introduce products such as GDP-linked or commodity price–linked bonds that might help manage seemingly important risks. Government attempts to introduce these products have been resisted because they do not generate sufficient fee income for private participants. The long-standing problem of the failure of financial markets to transfer risk from those in the developing countries who are less able to bear the risk of interest-rate and exchange-rate volatility to those in the developed countries who are more able to bear these risks has also remained unresolved.

Unregulated market forces have provided incentives not only for under-production of innovative financial products that support social goals but also for the creation of an abundance of financial products with little relevance to meeting social goals. There were incentives to exploit those who were financially unsophisticated and incentives to maximize transactions costs (e.g. in repeated refinancing of homes, excessive trading, or "churning"). By curtailing such socially unproductive innovation, better regulation may actually lead to more innovation that enhances societal well-being. Some of the areas in which innovation is badly needed are described below.

Government financial policy can also play an important catalytic role in the development of financial markets. Private financial markets have failed to make innovations that address many of the critical needs associated with ordinary citizens. In some cases, after the potential of such markets has been established, the private sector can take over. These innovations are important, both domestically and internationally, e.g., in improving the distribution of risk-bearing between developed and less-developed countries.

BOUNDARIES OF FINANCIAL REGULATION

Traditionally, regulation has been differentiated by institutional form: deposit-taking banks are regulated in a different way from non-banks. Insurance products are regulated by insurance regulators, but derivatives such as credit default swaps that have similar properties to insurance are unregulated. This represents the legacy of the past rather than an analytical approach to regulation and is vulnerable to regulatory arbitrage and in need of adjustment. Regulation needs to be comprehensive, with boundaries determined by the economic functions of financial institutions, not by what they are called or where they may be located.

Coverage should extend to all relevant institutions and instruments. The coherence of different regulatory frameworks needs to be considered when attempting to delineate the boundaries of regulation. Regulatory authorities need to coordinate seamless coverage across national and international capital markets, securities markets, and deposit takers. If regulation is not comprehensive and coherent, there is likely to be regulatory arbitrage with activity gravitating to the least regulated markets or to jurisdictions where regulations are most favorable. Comprehensive regulatory systems need to give priority to systemically important activities, institutions, and instruments. These should be subject to oversight, even if the intensity of regulation differs among them on the basis of their systemic importance.

However, there is no guarantee that all the practices that expose the financial sector and the economy to excessive risk can be properly monitored and regulated. As a result, regulation will have to put special emphasis on setting the right incentives (including strengthening financial responsibility so that failures in risk management are less likely to have adverse effects on others) in order to restrain excessively risky activities and to reduce the scope for adverse consequences.

At the international level, comprehensive coverage should eliminate the exposure of national financial systems to the possibility that some states might fail to implement effective regulation. At the same time, care should be taken that regulatory standards should not be an anti-competitive ploy by developed financial centers to maintain their positions attained in part through previous periods of regulatory and tax competition. (See below for further discussion).

More broadly, regulators also need to give special attention to financial institutions where governments are bearing implicit risk, either because of a bailout that may be necessary to protect the economy against systemic risk or because of the provision of (implicit or explicit) deposit insurance. The recent experience should make clear that any institution may have systemic significance. Indeed, the fact that some institutions were too big to be financially restructured has meant that protection has been provided not only to the institution but also to shareholders and other creditors. This suggests an even higher level of scrutiny for such institutions. There should be clear principles to determine what is considered systemically important, such as leverage, size, exposure to retail investors, and/or degree of correlation with other activities. Regulators must have comprehensive authority. There also needs to be a clear assessment of whether the concept of "too big to be financially resolved" has any validity, and if so, what the principles are that determine whether an institution is too big to be financially resolved. Regulation must occur continuously, on a day-to-day basis, while at the same time ensuring long-term consistency.

MICRO-PRUDENTIAL VS. MACRO-PRUDENTIAL REGULATION

Micro-prudential regulation, geared towards consumer protection, should apply to all financial institutions, with particular attention given to protection of unsophisticated "vulnerable" consumers. Macro-prudential regulation should be focused on key components of systemic risk: leverage, the failure of large, inter-connected institutions, and systemically important behavior and instruments and their interactions with the economic cycle. Both macro- and micro-prudential regulation should pay particular attention to potential risks undertaken by the government through implicit or explicit deposit insurance. Financial institutions that play a central role in the payments system thus need to be more intensely regulated through, for example, restrictions on risk-taking or capital adequacy standards. Some argue that imposing differential regulations may distort the financial system because of the implicit subsidies to such institutions on which appropriate regulations are not imposed. Restricting banks from engaging in certain risky activities does not mean that these risk services will not be provided; it simply means that they will be provided without the implicit subsidy associated with the risk of a government bailout. (See the discussion below.)

Macro-prudential regulation aims at reducing the pro-cyclicality of finance and its effects on the real economy. It does so by explicitly incorporating the effects of macroeconomic variables (growth, exchange rate, and interest rate movements) on financial risk, avoiding in particular the accumulation of systemic risks and changing crucial regulatory variables in a counter-cyclical fashion to discourage lending booms and prevent credit crunches.

Recessions that follow the sequence of lending booms and banking crises are often more severe and long lasting than recessions which originate in the real sector. This provides special impetus for regulation to be directed toward reducing the scope for financial market failures that are closely linked to economy-wide boom-bust cycles. Successful financial regulation should therefore not only ensure the safety and soundness of particular institutions but also enhance the stability of the macro economy.

Regulations should therefore focus more on those institutions most likely to have systemic consequences, which means those with the greatest leverage and size. But the experiences of this and previous crises suggest that it is difficult to tell which financial institutions will have systemic consequences, so that it is imperative to maintain some oversight over all activities, institutions, and instruments. Macroprudential regulation must thus go beyond banking institutions. This is particularly important given the tendency, and incentives, for financial market participants to engage in regulatory arbitrage through activities that have led to the creation of what has come to be called the "shadow banking system," which has a parallel in the creation of a "shadow insurance system." There should also be a special focus on aspects of the financial sector most likely to have significant consequences for the real economy. This entails protecting the payments system and ensuring the flow of credit.

Instruments should be regulated where their use might be harmful to vulnerable consumers or pose systemic risks to the economy or to the taxpayer. This could be achieved through a Financial Products Safety Commission to ascertain the safety and appropriate use of various financial instruments and practices for retail consumers. Alternatively, governments could create, within their existing regulatory structures, corresponding bodies that focus on consumer protection. It is important to recognize that seemingly safe instruments can have damaging consequences when their use changes, e.g., instruments used for hedging and insurance can also be used for speculation. Safety of financial products should thus be assessed not only in terms of their appropriateness in meeting the needs and objectives of retail consumers but also in terms of their impact on systemic behavior. Safety should be continuously reviewed with respect to prevailing practice and the consequences for product "safety." While great care should be taken in approving products for use by vulnerable consumers, all consumers need some protection. Many of the products marketed by American financial institutions were so complicated and complex that not even their creators seemed to be fully apprised of their risk properties.

Regulation must be dynamic, since instruments that initially appear to be safe can become dangerous with changing or growing use. Other instruments might initially appear to be excessively risky for some uses, but as their risk or complexity becomes understood and appropriate offsetting measures are devised, or as their safety is demonstrated in less regulated markets, they might be approved for specific uses in more regulated markets. A key part of supervision is the continuous monitoring and consideration of all instruments, institutions, markets, and behavior, with much more intense supervision and oversight of those with greater systemic importance.

Moreover, financial institutions will try to circumvent regulations. Regulators have to be especially attentive to the ever-present attempts at regulatory arbitrage and circumvention, including through the creation of arms-length special purpose vehicles. By definition, regulations reduce profits because they restrict potentially profitable actions. The fact that regulations are circumvented is no more an argument for abandoning regulation than the fact that tax laws are often circumvented is an argument for abandoning taxation. The fact that firms are always inventing ways of circumventing regulations means that governments have to view regulation as a dynamic process and provides an argument for legal frameworks that give regulators wide latitude to respond to the public interest.

Ring-Fencing

While there may be a case for differential regulation of financial market participants based on their sophistication, ability to bear risk, and the consequences that might arise from failure, it should also be recognized that in financial markets it is difficult to erect hermetically sealed barriers between the highly regulated actors posing systemic risks and those who do not. For instance, credit interlinkages are likely to remain. As a result, depending on the depth of a financial crisis, regulators may feel forced to rescue risky interlinked players in order to protect the interests of vulnerable participants and to avoid adverse systemic consequences. Typically, though, it is more "fiscally efficient" to directly bail out those who must be bailed out because of their direct systemic importance.

In order to prevent problems in the unregulated sector from spreading to the regulated sector when the government does not tightly regulate all financial institutions, the less regulated sector must be ring-fenced at least to some extent, with sensible controls on the extent of interaction with the more regulated sector. Governments need to be aware of the danger of contagion from one part of the financial system to others. Thus, the better and more comprehensive regulation, the more integrated (less segmented) the financial system can be.

The advantages of diversification provided by a large integrated firm or market may be more than offset by the risks of contagion, as a problem in one part of the economy spreads. This appears to be the case in the present crisis, especially in real estate. Had mortgages been centered in a specialized set of institutions, problems might have been contained, as they were in the U.S. savings-and-loan crisis in the 1980s.

Moreover, allowing highly risky activities to be undertaken within a regulated depository institution creates an unlevel playing field as a result of the potential subsidies that arise in the case of failure. Such distortions have been particularly evident in this crisis. In addition, they put the public finances at risk. (These issues are discussed further below.)

MACRO-PRUDENTIAL REGULATION

As pointed out above, the basic aim of macro-prudential regulation is to improve the stability of the macro economy, and particular at reducing the pro-cyclicality of finance and its effects on the real economy. The basic instrument is counter-cyclical regulation, but policies aimed at increasing the diversity of financial agents can also increase the stability of the system. A final set of issues relate to the management of the pro-cyclical pattern of capital flows that affect developing countries in particular and the role that capital account regulations can play to increase financial stability. They are considered later in the chapter, in relation to international issues.

COUNTER-CYCLICAL REGULATIONS

There is a long history of credit cycles, of which the current crisis is an example. In the boom, risk premiums decline and credit expands, largely based on collateral whose value increases with the expansion of credit. In the present crisis, as the rate of increase in real estate prices accelerated and the likelihood of a collapse increased, banks and other lenders lowered lending standards. There is by now ample evidence of this repeated pattern, suggesting that regulators should move more quickly to "lean against the wind." Counter-cyclical regulation can be an important part of economic strategies aimed at stabilizing the economy.

Existing capital adequacy regulations have actually had an adverse effect on stability and act in a pro-cyclical manner. When the economy goes into a downturn and banking institutions lack adequate provisions (reserves) for the risks they have assumed during the boom, bank capital declines due to the associated losses, and the bank is either forced to raise new capital at an unfavorable time or to cut back on lending. Too often, the only option is the latter. If many institutions are in a similar position, the result will be a credit crunch that reinforces the economic downturn.

Time-varying capital adequacy and provisioning requirements that rise and fall with the business cycle provide the best instrument of countercyclical macro-prudential regulation. These countercyclical capital adequacy and provisioning requirements can be based on simple rules which call, for instance, for an increase in capital requirements as the rate of growth of the assets of a bank increases or the rate of growth of a particular risky class of assets increases. Provisioning requirements automatically ensure that the bank sets aside more funds as it lends more. These regulations operate, in particular, as "speed bumps" that help dampen credit booms, reducing the likelihood that they will be followed by busts. As pointed out in the analysis of cross-border flows below, capital account regulations aimed at reducing capital inflows during booms can play a similar role in countries subject to pro-cyclical capital flows.

Variable risk weights used to ascertain appropriate capital adequacy standards can have strong incentive effects. Regulators need to be aware of distortions in capital allocation when provisioning and capital adequacy requirements do not accord well with actuarial risks. What is required is intense supervision and constant revaluation of the regulations. Maximum overall capital asset ratios should be imposed as a complement to accounting rules that adequately measure the associated risks through statistical accounting techniques that better estimate possible future losses than traditional accounting methods.

With current accounting practices which do not allow for statistical provisions, counter-cyclical capital adequacy requirements should be the preferred instrument. If statistical provisions are allowed, they may be preferable, as they follow the traditional principle that provisions should cover expected losses while capital should be able to cover unexpected events. This could be done, as the Spanish system introduced in 2000, by forcing financial institutions to make provisions equivalent to the expected losses from different groups of loans through a full business cycle, based on past experience. This principle also recognizes that the risk is incurred when loan disbursements are made, not when a loan is not paid (or expected not to be paid). In practice, however, counter-cyclical capital and provisioning requirements could be used as complements, as loan losses always have an unexpected component. Liquidity requirements can play an additional complementary role, particularly if they are also subject to counter-cyclical rules.

Regulation, and especially macro-prudential regulation, can have as important an effect on lending as open market operations or other central bank interventions. As an example of how macro-prudential and micro-prudential regulation could be combined, regulators and central banks might jointly agree to an annual rate of expansion in bank lending and to bands around that rate, above which a bank would be required to increase its capital adequacy or provisioning levels and below which it would be allowed to reduce those levels. The bands themselves might be adjusted in a way to help stabilize the economy.

If time-varying capital adequacy requirements had been in place, the magnitude of the previous boom and its inevitable crash would have been moderated. However, relating macro-prudential regulation to the rate of growth of bank lending would further enhance the temptation for banks to hide their own lending in associated off–balance sheet vehicles, like conduits and Special Investment Vehicles (SIVs). Regulators must prevent this by treating all such arms-length vehicles on a consolidated basis.

A series of micro-prudential regulations can also have macro-prudential effects. For instance, during booms, increasing the loan-to-value ratios for mortgages and requiring larger monthly payments of outstanding credit card debts will help reduce an excessive growth of these types of lending. Provisioning standards could also be raised for sectors experiencing credit booms. And, as pointed out below, managing the currency mismatches of lending can also provide an essential tool to reduce credit risks in countries facing pro-cyclical capital flows.

The Advantages of Diversification

Regulation should be more focused on the capacity of the financial system as a whole to bear and allocate risks and where this is best done rather than solely on measures of individual firm risks. Risk is not just about assets; it is about how the assets are funded and how they are used. Regulation of systemic risks needs to include an assessment of funding liquidity.

Financial liquidity and stability requires diversity of action and opinion. If all firms respond in the same way (e.g., trying to sell the same asset at the same time), markets may exhibit extreme volatility. It is important that regulators do what they can to preserve natural diversity, especially in the face of enhanced transparency, common accounting standards, and the increasing comprehensiveness of regulation.

The benefit of diversity is another argument in favor of a return to more specialized, simpler institutions and the segmentation of markets, perhaps with a return to the "public utility" aspect of banking for core deposit-taking institutions and regulatory segmentation of institutions into areas such as retail banking, long-term savings institutions, and wholesale investment banking. Each function could then be regulated to discourage it from holding risks it does not have a natural capacity to hold and manage.[2] Alternatively, specific regulations tailored to the different financial activities undertaken within a universal banking structure, or the subsidiaries of a bank holding company, could be introduced to equivalent effect.

The virtue of differentiated regulatory structures and standards for different kinds of financial institutions has to be offset against the risks of regulatory arbitrage. There needs to be systemic oversight over the entire financial system to make sure that there is not extensive regulatory arbitrage.

MICRO-PRUDENTIAL REGULATORY ISSUES

RESTRICTING EXCESSIVELY RISKY PRACTICES

It is clear that the banks have engaged in excessively risky practices. They have had excessive leverage and traded in highly risky credit default swaps without adequate assessment of counterparty risk. Trading in subprime mortgages and complex securities based on these mortgages exposed banks to risks that they did not fully assess.

This crisis illustrates the risks of excessive leverage, which yields high returns to equity when markets are going up but exposes them to huge losses when markets are declining. If a financial institution has a 30 to 1 leverage, just a 3% decline in asset prices wipes out all the value of the owners' equity.

Unrealistic market expectations of returns to equity, often in the range of 20% per annum, typify the market pressures that existed before the crisis. Such returns can only be achieved if there is: (a) lack of competition or (b) excessive risk taking. Such returns in the financial sector should be the subject of intensive scrutiny and supervision. If they are a result of insufficient competition, strong antitrust actions need to be undertaken (see below). If they are the result of excessive risk-taking based on the expectation of a government guarantee, then they should be directly proscribed by the regulator.

The extent of the risk associated with any particular action may depend on the state of the business cycle. The same loan-to-value ratio in a bubble poses greater risk than in more normal times. This provides a further rationale (besides economic stability) for counter-cyclical capital adequacy and/or provisioning requirements discussed in the previous section.

Regulators should not, however, rely just on capital adequacy standards, even cyclically and risk-adjusted capital adequacy standards. One reason is that such restrictions may, in fact, induce greater risk taking, because while the firm may have more "wealth" at risk, there is a diminution in the franchise value of the bank as an ongoing concern, so there is less to lose in a bet that threatens the bank's survival.

Regulators also need to be attentive to managerial incentives and who bears the risks of failure. This is especially so in the current crisis when the government may have provided large fractions of the capital of a bank, but governments have chosen not to exercise adequate control. While the capital provided by the government enhances the bank's buffer against shocks, the impact on incentives may be far less, as bank executives focus their attention on private shareholders or even on the consequences to themselves. Thus, when the U.S. government provided more funds in the form of preferred shares, banks used the money in part to fund bonuses, share buybacks, and dividends, even though such actions significantly increased the risk of future problems.

Risk adjustments can also discriminate against developing countries and contribute to systemic instability. Under the Basel I accord, short-term lending was treated as less risky than long-term lending. Lending to developing countries, even those that seemed to have a record of economic stability, was treated as riskier than lending to more developed countries. These adjustments resulted in extensive reliance on short-term lending to developing countries contributing to the crisis of 1997–1998.

Governments, especially in developing countries, may want to consider other restrictions such as quantitative restrictions and/or higher provisions on the fraction of bank portfolios that can be allocated to certain sectors prone to speculative activity, such as real estate. This may not only lead to greater stability but also ensure greater financing for infrastructure or employment-related investments on a longer-term basis.

Countries that allow banks to own equity shares may experience greater volatility because a sudden decrease in stock prices can induce a credit contraction. Specific, appropriate regulation should thus be exercised if banks invest in equity shares.

Some problems in earlier crises were a result of foreign exchange mismatches. Regulations should place strict limits on uncovered foreign exchange exposures. Attention should be paid to indirect foreign exchange exposure, that is, loans to firms that have foreign exchange exposures. Since such exposure is cyclically related, such regulations may play an important role in macro-economic instability, and can be viewed as part of macro-prudential regulation.

Similarly, there should be restrictions on engaging in swaps and other insurance and derivative products other than to hedge or mitigate existing risks. Banks, with their implicit or explicit government guarantees, should be prevented from activities that may significantly increase their individual and systemic risks.

Countries that allowed the balance sheets of domestic banks to grow beyond the size of their economy will have difficulty in meeting guarantees should the banks fail, or can only do so at great cost to the rest of society. It is thus necessary that either: (i) a global deposit insurance fund be created, funded by fees on banks or a tax on all cross-border deposits and backed by the governments of the depositors or (ii) depositors in foreign banks not explicitly insured by the host country recognize that those deposits are not insured. The provision by the host country of deposit insurance should only extend to separately capitalized subsidiaries of foreign banks, with strong restrictions on the payout of capital to the holding company and close oversight by host country regulators.

REGULATING SECURITIES MARKETS

Banks are only one part of the modern financial system, and many non-bank operations in the securities market have contributed to the current crisis. Excessive volatility in securities markets can have adverse effects throughout the financial system.

Securitization held open the promise of risk diversification and access to new sources of funding. But it also opened up new information asymmetries and avenues of inappropriate behavior by investors who did not possess the ability to bear the risks or could not evaluate them appropriately since they did not have the relevant knowledge of the underlying assets available to the originators. Markets, regulators, and the models used by bankers, credit rating agencies, and investors to assess risks overestimated the benefits of risk diversification and underestimated the costs of the information asymmetries and herd behavior by investors.

Securitization has also presented new problems for debt restructuring that were already evident in the response to problems that arose earlier in the debt crises of the late 20th century. It was far easier to restructure the sovereign debts in the Latin American crises of the 1980s than in the East Asian and Latin American crises of the late 1990s and early years of this decade. In the present crisis, restructuring has been made more difficult by explicit restrictions imposed by the securities that were issued (presumably to give more confidence in these securities). Further problems have been created by complicated conflicts of interest: where the interests of service providers, nominally responsible for the restructuring, may not coincide with those of mortgage holders; where there are conflicts of interest between those who hold first and second mortgages; and where the service providers are often owned by those who hold the second mortgage. There are large social costs associated with these difficulties in restructuring that become particularly acute in an economic crisis and which parties promoting securitization may not fully internalize.

Originators of securities should be required to hold a stake of at least 10% in each securities issue they underwrite. While this might reduce the capacity for future securitization, it would also substantially reduce the potential for systemic risks associated with structured products and would encourage higher underwriting and lending standards.

REGULATION OF CREDIT DERIVATIVES AND SWAPS

Since the default of a large corporation can have far greater monetary implications than the size of any of its outstanding liabilities, it may be prudent for lenders to hedge the risk of default of the company affecting its suppliers, dealers, pensioners, stores local to the employees, etc., so that the outstanding value of credit default swaps (CDS) may be larger than the liability of the direct creditors. However, there are systemic implications of a large CDS market, especially where there is no centralized clearinghouse or regulated exchange trading. As the AIG episode illustrated, a failure of one institution can have a cascade of effects, and it may be very difficult to evaluate fully the nature of counterparty risk.

Hence regulatory agencies should be authorized to require any CDS transactions (singly or in total) that it considers to be of systemic importance to comply with a range of requirements, including registration, centralized clearing, and, where appropriate to the risks being taken, margin and capital requirements.

When there is extensive exposure to over-the-counter (OTC) CDSs, as noted above, the effective exercise of market discipline requires the disclosure of net positions so that the market can evaluate the nature of the counterparty risk. Revelation of gross exposures will not suffice, in particular because details of contracts may mean that positions are not really fully netted out. Thus, while the regulator should have a preference for exchange-traded instruments relative to OTC instruments, if the latter are approved, there should be adequate transparency in the form of mandated and regular reporting to the regulator, and aggregate information should be put in the public domain as determined by the regulator.

Comprehensive regulation entails ensuring that equivalent instruments be treated with equivalent regulation. Thus, for example, to the extent that a CDS is equivalent to an insurance contract, it should be subject to equivalent regulation.

INVESTOR PROTECTION AND ACCESS

Predatory Lending and Usury

Regulating predatory lending is primarily a matter of consumer/ investor protection, but, as this crisis has shown, it is also a matter of risk management. The elimination of usury restrictions has been advocated on the grounds that it encourages risk taking. But it may have resulted in excessive risk-taking and the abuse of ill-informed borrowers. The excessive returns garnered by such lenders have contributed to the bloating of the financial sector.

The subprime mortgage market provided examples of predatory lending, but there have been other abusive practices as well. Regulators need to be attentive to the variety of forms that circumvention can take, e.g., through rent-to-own and payday loans.[3]

Recent years have seen particular abuses in regulations covering the use of credit cards. Such practices have flourished, in part because of anti-competitive behavior, which has helped generate above market returns. Moreover, abusive lending practices lead to high returns to lending and have contributed to a build-up of excessive household debt. The misery of the ill-informed borrower is compounded by the recourse by lenders to recovery agents who use unregulated and often illicit means of loan recovery. Some governments have introduced measures to discourage such predatory practices, such as making abusive credit contracts unenforceable.

Even when lending practices may not be predatory, mortgage and other financial products may impose excessive risk or costs on borrowers. An important function of a Financial Products Safety Commission or a similar body within a broader regulatory structure is to assess the safety and appropriateness of financial products for individuals in different circumstances.

Access Regulation

Financial regulation can and should be used to affect lending patterns where social and private returns may differ. It can help direct lending into socially desirable areas and discourage lending where private benefits exceed social costs.

For instance, many countries have enacted regulations to prevent racial and ethnic discrimination and have passed legislation to encourage lending to underserved groups. In some countries, mandates for lending to underserved segments have played an important role and have even proven profitable in the long-term. While pressure has been exerted on developing countries to eliminate such requirements, the U.S. Community Reinvestment Act is actually a successful example of such practices. Because information is at the heart of banking, requirements that banks open up branches in underserved parts of a country can also be an important instrument of development. Negative and positive "priority" lending may be most effective when broad based, leaving the private sector with the strongest incentives to find the best commercial opportunities within those constraints.

Regulations affecting the direction of lending can also be used for macro-prudential reasons. While lending to the real estate sector can have a number of social benefits, it is also a common source of excessive lending and asset market bubbles. Consequently, limits to real estate–related lending, such as loan-to-value limits on mortgage lending, should be instituted. These limits should be counter-cyclical, rising in a boom and falling in a crash.

Restricting lending, e.g., to the real estate sector, may also be an important instrument in encouraging lending to other sectors. Such restrictions may enhance stability, development, and job creation. This is an arena in which regulatory tools should be accompanied by other instruments of financial policy. (See the discussion below.)

REGULATING COMPETITION

Competition policy (antitrust) is one area of government regulation that applies to all sectors of the economy—including the financial sector—but inadequacies in such regulation may be particularly manifest, and costly, in the financial sector.

Failure to enforce effective antitrust policies has led to excessive concentration in the financial sector. Lack of competition is evident in supra-normal profits, in excessive fees, in other anti-competitive practices, and most importantly in this context, in banks that have grown too big to fail.

Even more worrisome is the claim by some governments that certain banks are too big to be financially restructured (or "resolved") (TBTR). The argument is put forward that any resolution entailing losses to shareholders or bondholders would cause such massive market disturbance and/or impair the ability of banks to raise capital in the future that the costs exceed the benefits. In such cases, taxpayers must pick up a much larger part of the cost of financial restructuring. They provide money that otherwise should have come from shareholders or bond-holders. Financial restructurings may be close to zero-sum games, im-plying that if the losses of shareholders and bondholders are reduced, the losses to taxpayers are increased by a corresponding amount.

Not only will such institutions face distorted incentives towards excessive risk taking since they know that the government will bear the costs of large losses, but the implicit subsidy given to these institu-tions also produces market distortions. Under current arrangements, knowing that they are too big to fail or to be financially resolved, large banks have an unwarranted competitive advantage over smaller banks because of the implicit insurance.

One of the original motivations for antitrust laws was a concern for excessive concentration of political power. The ability of the finan-cial sector to obtain favorable laws and regulations, at great cost to the rest of society, and to obtain large bailouts and to do so repeatedly, combined with evidence of large campaign contributions and heavy lobbying, suggests cause for concern.

While the increase in market concentration may be a natural con-sequence of the winnowing out of firms in the context of a major economic downturn, the problem has been exacerbated by the way some governments have managed bailouts. Disproportionate amounts have gone to large and dominant firms. In providing bailout funds, the impact on the competitive structure of the financial sector should be an important criterion.

Too-Big-to-Be-Resolved Financial Institutions

When faced with the challenge of restructuring large multifaceted in-stitutions on the verge of insolvency, public officials have chosen delib-erate forbearance on the grounds that public control of these institutions (through nationalization or intervention—in the latter case, putting them into conservatorship, in U.S. terminology) and/or inducing a fi-nancial restructuring that entailed a loss to shareholders or bondhold-ers, even those that are not secured, would produce catastrophic disruption of financial markets and the real economy. Some have sug-gested that the sheer size and complexity of these institutions means that changing organizational forms would start a run on other institutions heavily intertwined with the behemoth institutions on the threshold of insolvency.

Whether or not these arguments are valid, if governments adopt this principle, it means in essence that society is faced with a policy regime where officials claim they cannot protect government finances and taxpayers from the excesses of the TBTR firms. A strategy of allowing a financial institution to embed itself so deeply into the fabric of the economy that it cannot be permitted to be resolved puts society in a position of great fiscal danger. It no longer has control of the scale of fiscal losses that can be imposed upon it by financial institutions' managers.

This puts the management of TBTR institutions in a very powerful position incompatible with wider social goals. The problems are far worse than with too-big-to-fail (TBTF) institutions. In some countries, even at present, the scale of these institutions has reached such a magnitude that the value of guarantees on liabilities is drawn into question.

The TBTR regime goes beyond TBTF, where critical functions of restructured institutions have to be preserved. These can be preserved while making shareholders and bondholders bear the costs of their mistakes (though in some cases, their mistakes are so large that the government may be required to provide additional funding to maintain the firm as an ongoing institution). A TBTR regime implies that management and creditors are immune from the consequences of their actions or inaction—particularly in relation to risk management. There is insufficient market discipline, since TBTR status removes risk from creditors, giving these institutions an advantage that enables them to further increase their size. A policy regime such as this is not consistent with a market economy that performs its social functions well in the longer term.

Standard antitrust policies should be implemented, but the usual metrics for excessive economic concentration (share of the top four firms in the market, or the ability to determine market prices) may not be totally adequate in the context of financial markets. These criteria may need to be supplemented by an assessment of whether the financial institution is at risk of being too big to fail or too big to be financially restructured. Such large institutions should be broken up and limited in size so that they are not too big to fail and certainly not too big to be financially resolved. There is little evidence of significant economies of scale or scope, at least of sufficient magnitude, to warrant the risks imposed on the economy and the public finances.

But such measures need to be supplemented by financial sector regulatory measures. Any large bank that is not broken up should have stronger capital adequacy requirements than other banks and face more stringent restrictions in each of the areas discussed so far (e.g., on the admissible set of incentive structures, on transparency, and on the kinds of risks that they can undertake, such as lower leverage). Because of the greater cost to government of problems in these institutions, they should also face increased premiums for deposit insurance.

REGULATING OTHER PLAYERS

Financial markets have become more complex over time. Finance is provided by banks and through securities markets. There are a host of other actors, some of whom have played an important role in the current crisis and have become the subject of extensive controversy. In particular, there are two non-traditional groups of financial institutions that require special attention: rating agencies and sovereign wealth funds.

Rating Agencies

Credit rating agencies (CRAs) were supposed to play a key role in financial markets by reducing information asymmetries between issuers and investors. Their role has expanded with financial globalization and received additional importance in Basel II, which incorporates the CRAs' ratings into the rules for assessing credit risk.

However, the role of rating agencies in the present crisis has been subject to serious criticism due to the generous ratings given to complex financial instruments backed by subprime mortgages. The risk assessments of rating agencies have been highly pro-cyclical and tend to react to the realization of risks rather than to risk build-up, in relation to both sovereign and corporate risk. The risk models of CRAs rely, to a large extent, on market-determined variables like equity prices and credit spreads, thus exacerbating pro-cyclicality.

Since CRAs are paid by those they are asked to evaluate, they are subject to a clear conflict of interest that has undermined confidence. Moreover, the provision of consulting services to their clients presents another conflict of interest similar to that forbidden to accounting firms in the United States. It is no less problematic in the case of rating agencies, and these should be forbidden.

This is not the first instance of widespread failures of the CRAs. Their failures were widely noted in the 1997–1998 financial crisis, and it is widely thought that the late and marked downgrades to below investment grade in many cases contributed greatly to the depth of the crisis.

Inaccurate assessments may have other adverse effects beyond exacerbating cyclical fluctuations. As assessments of creditworthiness by CRAs came to be viewed as authoritative in financial markets, such ratings often adversely affected financing for developing countries. Indeed, they may have contributed to the fact that there appears to be "excess" returns to a diversified portfolio of sovereign bonds, i.e., such bonds are underpriced.

In spite of the fact that CRAs play such a large role in financial markets, they are essentially unregulated. While greater oversight is required, there is no set of reforms that have received general support and which would convincingly resolve the problem. One reform, designed to remove the conflict of interest, would impose a charge on all security issues to be used to finance one or more ratings.

Greater transparency in the way that rating agencies discuss and present their analyses, clarifying assumptions made and the sensitivity of the results to these assumptions, should enhance the functioning of financial markets. In addition, rating agencies should be required to provide information concerning their overall past performance, and/or an independent government agency should provide such information, which would enhance "positive" competition among rating agencies.

Rating agencies should be forced to abandon their obscure and non-comparable rating systems and provide a quantitative assessment of the probability of default. The accuracy of these forecasts can then be assessed.

Part of the problem is caused by the small oligopoly market structure of the credit rating agencies, which means that ratings failures do not lead to significant market discipline. Many investors, and hence borrowers, are required by their investment bylaws to obtain a rating from each of the main agencies. It may be necessary, therefore, for the government to impose discipline by penalizing rating failures, e.g., losing the "accreditation" for a certain period of time after evidence of systematic and significant failures in assessment. But even this remedy has problems. Since ratings are correlated, there is a chance that all agencies will lose their accreditation at the same time. Knowing that it would be hard to enforce such a policy in such a circumstance may encourage rating agencies to maintain ratings that are similar to each other.

Given the difficulties of resolving the problems posed by CRAs, it is important that regulators and others charged with risk management reduce their reliance on external ratings. Rating agencies proved to be no less pro-cyclical than market prices, and their use by regulators has added to the pro-cyclicality of bank lending.

Problems with individual ratings need to be viewed in the broader context of the provision of information in the financial sector. In the Enron and WorldCom scandals, conflicts of interest in the stock and bond research and ratings provided by analysts paid by investment banks drew extensive criticism. In the recent food and energy crises, information provided by some investment banks may have simultaneously enriched those providing the information and contributed to those crises. While the reforms concerning analysts' pay were a move in the right direction, they do not go far enough. There should be disclosure at least to the regulator (as is already the case in some countries) of the positions of investment banks and others capable of "moving" markets, to at least identify potential conflicts of interest.

Sovereign Wealth Funds

Earlier conventional wisdom argued that ownership did not matter, so long as it was not the government of the country in whose domain the assets resided. Developing countries were urged to privatize state-owned assets, paying little attention to the identity of the buyer, even if, in some cases, it was a foreign government or government-owned firm. It seemed permissible for a foreign government to own a country's assets but not the country's own government. As entities owned and controlled by foreign governments have taken more active roles in purchasing assets in developed countries, these views have evolved, creating uncertainty over the rules of the game. Whatever rules are devised and agreed upon should be universally and fairly applied.

There may be particular industries or sectors where ownership matters. Governments should agree on these sectors and make them public. If national security provides a rationale for ownership restrictions in one country, there should be a presumption that it provides a rationale for similar limitations on ownership in other countries. If ownership matters, one should be as concerned by aberrant private sector behavior as by that of a government-owned enterprise. Indeed, some have suggested that governments may be more responsible investors than private investors, precisely because of the greater degree of public accountability expected.

Some have suggested that a special code of conduct be imposed on sovereign wealth funds, including provisions relating to transparency and disclosure, including disclosure of the sovereign wealth fund's business model. Others have argued this is just window dressing on the part of countries that want the funds but realize the political sensitivities: almost any action can be cloaked within a business rationale. While transparency and disclosure may be helpful, it is unlikely that it would solve the problem. So too with a broader voluntary code of conduct.

Any conditions or requirements imposed on sovereign wealth funds should be symmetrically imposed on private-sector investors. The point is reinforced by the growing blurring of the line between private and public investors, with the bulk of the capital of many Western banks now being provided by governments.

Moreover, restrictions on sovereign wealth funds may be relatively meaningless, so long as there is no comprehensive disclosure of ownership. Ownership stakes could be mediated through third parties (such as hedge funds) without disclosure. If governments are concerned about ownership, there has to be appropriately comprehensive disclosure.

If there are certain behaviors of the foreign owner that are a source of concern, those behaviors should be restricted, whether on the part of private or government entities. Worries about their behavior are thus symptomatic of a lack of confidence in the overall regulatory regime. Countries should identify the inadequacies in their regulatory structures and seek to remedy them.

FINANCIAL RESTRUCTURING

All governments need to have adequate legal frameworks to deal with situations where firms cannot meet their obligations to creditors (i.e., bankruptcy). Such laws need to balance the rights and interests of creditors and debtors and the consequences for economic efficiency, both ex ante (i.e., the impact on incentives to assess creditworthiness) and ex post (i.e., the impact on incentives on the part of debtors to comply with their obligations, of creditors to monitor effectively, and of both sides to enter into timely renegotiations when problems arise). They should create a framework for fair negotiation among the parties involved, leading to rapid and efficient bankruptcy proceedings if such negotiations fail. It is better to have clarity about such matters prior to the signing of contracts so that parties know more fully their rights and responsibilities.

Some countries, such as the U.S., have corporate bankruptcy provisions that allow for speedy resolution, giving firms a fresh start in the belief that it is in the broader interests of society to maintain jobs and the firm as an ongoing concern. Keeping a family in their house is equally important, as is giving families overburdened with debt a fresh start.

Governments should consider passing a "home owners Chapter 11" (analogous to Chapter 11 in the U.S. bankruptcy code for corporations).

The bankruptcy of large numbers of firms in the midst of a crisis presents special challenges. Delays in resolution have large externalities, giving rise to adverse macro-economic effects. Furthermore, many countries do not have adequate resources to deal with such massive problems, which are complicated by high levels of interdependency (i.e., assessing the net worth of one firm for purposes of bankruptcy may depend on the resolution of the debts for other firms). Governments need to consider passing a "super Chapter 11" to facilitate expedited restructuring in the event of a systemic crisis where there are large numbers of defaults such as occurred in several developing countries after their financial crises.

Banks and other financial institutions present special problems for debt restructuring because of the stake of the government, through implicit and explicit deposit insurance, because of the externalities that may result from the failure of such institutions, and because the government does not want to wait until the institution has no capacity to repay creditors. Doing so can give rise to especially large adverse incentive effects, e.g., "gambling on resurrection." It is necessary for governments to have a legal framework for prompting corrective action, including intervening in such institutions (placing them into a conservatorship) and other discretionary powers of resolution.

In the current crisis, some governments claimed that they did not have legal authority to deal effectively with institutions whose failure might pose systemic risk. It is clear not only that any such institutions should be highly regulated but also that there need to be effective mechanisms for financial restructuring. Such mechanisms should apply to any financial institution judged to have the potential to cause systemic consequences, including financial services holding companies, investment banks, and insurance companies. Foreign firms operating within a country that have systemic consequences present special challenges, and there is accordingly a strong argument to require domestic incorporation. (These arguments are in addition to the other arguments, discussed below.) Such mechanisms need to recognize the rights not only of shareholders and bondholders but also those likely to be adversely affected by a failure of the institution.

Converting long-term debt holders into shareholders increases the financial viability of the bank and should enhance market confidence, not weaken it. There is very limited if any evidence that, in the process of conservatorship, shareholders' loss of value will generate market disturbance.

Of course, a disorderly process of bankruptcy in which the integrity of the payments mechanism is not protected can give rise to large externalities. Government powers of resolution should extend to allowing a quick restructuring of the large financial institutions, which would facilitate the maintenance of the integrity of the payments system but allow, for instance, an associated real estate or hedge fund within the institution to go into bankruptcy.

The need for using such powers of resolution will be reduced if governments adopt strategies to limit the absolute size of financial institutions. In addition, extensive examination of large institutions on an ongoing basis can prepare officials for controlled restructuring. There is not a basis for allowing these large institutions any degree of opacity vis-à-vis regulators, who must always be prepared for the contingency of a resolution.

Incentives, Guarantees and Insurance, and Bailouts

Guarantees and insurance (implicit and explicit) distort incentives since they are designed to eliminate the risk of loss; the higher potential gain from more risky behavior accrues to the recipient of the guarantee, while the larger losses are absorbed by the guarantor. Concern about these distortions has been increased by the massive increase in government guarantees in the present crisis.

The recent bailouts have also raised issues of conflicts of interest and divergences between the interests of firm managers and of those providing capital. The provision of capital by some governments without exercising control over how the capital is used exacerbates the usual incentive problems that arise when there is a separation between ownership and control. The much criticized behavior of banks taking money intended to recapitalize them and paying it out in bonuses and dividends instead is explicable in terms of the differences in interests between those making the decisions (the bank officers) and the public providing the money. The risks should have been apparent (see the discussion in Chapter 2).

Some governments have used guarantees and insurance as part of bailout packages that lacked sufficient transparency concerning the risk of loss; it has not always been clear that governments have been adequately compensated for the risk borne by the public. Such non-transparency should always be discouraged, but some of these programs may be particularly costly in this crisis because they create perverse incentives on the part of banks to restructure mortgages.

However, in times of economic crisis, guarantees and insurance may be part of a government's crisis response in order to stimulate counter-cyclical economic activity and to prevent runs on banks. In some cases, issuing government guarantees may even be a strategy to attract individuals to make investments (or to induce banks to finance investments) with relatively high risk but with highly positive long-term economic, social, or ecological effects. However, there is some presumption that providing guarantees for new loans or creating new lending facilities may be a more effective way of stimulating such investments than buying non-performing assets from banks or even providing new funds to existing banks for recapitalization. Adverse incentive effects can be mitigated by providing only partial insurance guarantees.

While the main mandate of central banks is to provide liquidity, when this involves accepting risky assets as collateral on a non-recourse basis, it amounts to an insurance policy on the losses associated with these assets. When insurance premiums on such guarantees and insurance are not set at the appropriate level, they represent a non-transparent transfer, and such non-transparent transfers on the part of central banks and governments should be discouraged. Typically, such guarantees, bailouts, and insurance represent a large transfer of wealth from ordinary individuals to those who are, on average, better off. If there are particular groups that might be adversely affected by a financial restructuring and deserve to be protected, it is far better to target assistance to such parties. The non-transparent bailouts, guarantees, and insurance undermine confidence in government and central banks, strengthen the case against an independent central bank (see the discussion above), and may create a political backlash, hampering government's ability to deal with the present crisis if it proves to be as long lasting as some believe it may.

REGULATORY INSTITUTIONS

Regulatory Failure

It is not enough to have good regulations; they have to be enforced. The failures in this crisis are not just a failure of regulation but of regulatory institutions that did not always effectively implement or enforce the regulations. In this crisis, the regulatory performance of many central banks has been far from stellar. They did not adequately enforce and implement the regulations at their disposal, and they did not alert governments to the need for additional regulatory authority or restructuring authority when existing authority was not adequate.

All human institutions are fallible, and it may happen again, especially if those who are appointed to oversee the regulatory system do not believe that regulation has a role or are not fully sympathetic with the roles that it should play.

At the same time, it is clear that regulatory structures can be designed in ways that reduce the scope for the failure of regulatory institutions. Regulators may be under pressure during a boom. While the regulator is supposed "to take away the punch bowl just before the party gets going," pressures are often brought to bear to continue the party, since so many are making so much money doing so. Specious arguments are brought forward—such as the impossibility of identifying a bubble until it breaks. This is true, but it is possible to ascertain an increasing probability of a bubble as prices relative to incomes attain historically high or even unprecedented levels.

Another specious argument is that regulators or central banks do not have instruments with which to deflate a bubble. The instruments available—increasing margin requirements in the case of a stock market bubble or decreasing loan-to-value ratios in the case of a real estate bubble—have been analyzed elsewhere in this report.

Still a third specious argument that was put forward before the crisis is that it is less expensive to repair the damage caused by the breaking of a bubble than to dampen the bubble itself. The current crisis has clearly shown that this is not the case.

In light of this pressure, it may be necessary for part of the regulatory structure to be "hard wired," limiting the discretion available to regulators and supervisors. Counter-cyclical provisioning and capital adequacy requirements of the kind discussed in previous sections should be rule-based, while adjustments to regulation due to evolution of financial practices and innovation will require monitoring and discretion in adjusting regulations as appropriate.

Capture and Voice

Regulatory institutions have to be created with recognition of the risks of capture by the interests and perspectives of those being regulated, and they must ensure that the users of finance—such as small and medium-sized businesses, pensioners, consumers, and perhaps other stakeholders—are given voice. For instance, pensioners who are likely to see their hard-earned pension funds disappear as a result of poor regulation should have a stronger voice in regulatory structures. Those who benefit from the continuation of a bubble often have excessive influence on the regulatory institutions as presently constituted.

The creation of a specific financial regulator (with appropriate governance structures) whose mandate is to ascertain the safety and appropriate use of various financial products may reduce the likelihood of regulatory capture.

Regulation and Political Processes

Regulation is part of the political process; failures in public governance contribute to failures in regulatory design. When the political process is unduly influenced by campaign contributions and other forms of lobbying by the financial sector, failures in the design of financial regulations become more likely. In some countries, "revolving doors" that allow individuals easy movement between jobs in government and the private sector and other pecuniary and non-pecuniary considerations present problems compromising the integrity, adequacy, and appropriateness of financial regulation, supervision, and enforcement.

Regulatory design needs to be able to resist attempts by the industry to influence regulators and to divert them from their core responsibilities of consumer and investor protection and systemic stability. Much can be done to design regulatory systems that have built-in resistance to capture, such as reliance on simple and transparent rules regarding the regulation of instruments that are potentially of systemic significance. The design of regulatory governance can also reduce the scope for capture, ensuring that those who are likely to be hurt by a failure of regulation rather than those who benefit from weak regulation dominate the regulatory process.

"Regulatory capture" occurs not just through financial contributions but also through ideas. Many of the ideas that persuaded regulators to limit regulation simultaneously enhanced the profits of the financial sector. "Revolving doors" not only provide perverse incentives but also facilitate this form of capture. Governments should put in place strong restrictions on revolving doors. Today, there are experts in finance and economics that neither work for nor are indebted to the financial sector, and greater reliance should be placed on them. More generally, those from the financial sector, even though they are familiar with industry practices and perspectives, often do not understand the systemic consequences of policies and even less the implications for the broader economy. Reliance on experts from the financial sector may, as a result, lead governments to have an excessively "partial equilibrium" approach to policy. This crisis can be seen, in part, as a result of excessive attention being given to these forms of expertise.

Personnel

Many regulatory bodies face difficulties in attracting qualified personnel: the battle between the regulator and the regulated might seem to be unfair from the start, given the high salaries paid in the private financial sector. But the skills and talents necessary for creating new products and circumventing existing regulations and accounting standards are different from those required for assessing the safety and soundness of financial institutions or the safety and efficacy of particular financial products. Nonetheless, it may be desirable, or even necessary, to link the salaries of the regulators to those in the financial sector, paid for by a financial sector tax.

Regulatory Structure

Much of the discussion over regulatory design has focused on the problem of assignments of responsibilities, e.g., should there be a single regulatory authority for the entire financial sector? Old models of regulatory structure have been failing because different institutions have been providing services formerly associated with other institutions. Securities markets, insurance firms, and futures exchanges all provide opportunities for market participants to speculate on the outcomes of particular events (securities, defaults). Should, for instance, responsibility be assumed by the central banks? While there appears to be no single model appropriate for all countries, there are certain principles that should guide the design of the regulatory structure.

While different countries, at different stages of development, may find different structures better in meeting their overall needs, one possible structure entails two apex regulatory institutions working closely together: a New Central Bank (NCB), focusing on macroeconomic issues, and a Financial Regulatory Authority (FRA), focusing on micro-issues, closely coordinated with each other so that, for instance, the NCB would be aware of the macroeconomic consequences of the actions taken by the FRA. This is especially important because micro-prudential regulations have macroeconomic consequences. The FRA would have several subcommissions under it: a Securities and Exchange Commission, an Insurance Commission, a Financial Products Safety Commission, an Accounting Oversight Commission, and a Financial Systems Stability Commission (which among other things would look at the interlinkages among financial institutions and the vulnerability of the failure of one to that of another). It would have cross-cutting committees to ensure that similar functions performed by different institutions are treated similarly. The Financial Systems Stability Commission could impose high margin requirements or large down payments for products sold to retail customers if it felt that there was growing excess leverage in the economy or in the market. The Accounting Oversight Commission would ensure that the information provided by firms is not misleading and represents the best estimate of the overall state of the firm, including its vulnerability. It might, over time, develop a broader set of metrics that might be of use to investors and other regulators. It would seek to prohibit off–balance sheet exposures but recognize that financial institutions have been creative, both in their accounting and in devising ways of circumventing regulations and accounting standards, and be given broad discretion to impose additional reporting requirements and to employ conservative methodologies in the valuation of risk or dilution. For example, while there may be controversies over valuing stock options for purposes of reporting at the time they are issued, given the objectives of accounting standards and the importance of developing good incentive structures, methodologies which might be at risk of overestimating the value of the dilution are to be preferred to those that underestimate the value.

GLOBAL REGULATION AND REGULATION OF CROSS-BORDER FINANCE AND CAPITAL

This crisis in global financial markets differs from all previous crises in its global reach. The new financial products and procedures that caused difficulty in the U.S. were exported on a large scale, with severe consequences for the importing countries. While it may not be the only source of the problems facing some European countries, it is a major contributor. As the crisis has evolved, there has been a breakdown of trust in financial institutions. Citizens no longer trust the regulators supposed to regulate them, and regulators in one country no longer trust that regulators in other countries, even those with seemingly good institutions, are doing their jobs properly.

Moreover, the policies pushed by the international financial institutions (financial market liberalization and capital market liberalization) are now seen as having contributed to the crisis and its rapid spread around the world. This has undermined confidence in these institutions, the advice that they proffered, and the conditionalities that they imposed, raising questions about the suitability of excess reliance on these institutions for the disbursement of funds to developing countries, as already noted in Chapter 2. New international regulations will thus be paramount in the response to the crisis. There is a need for a new approach to comprehensive global regulation.

Global Coordination

As financial markets become global, it is imperative to have global coordination of regulation. Failure of regulation by one country can have adverse effects on others. This is especially important since responsibility for bailouts remains at the national level. If countries cannot rely on the safety of the financial products exported by a country, they may restrict the purchase of these products by their citizens and financial institutions; if they cannot trust the safety and soundness of other countries' financial institutions, they will have to restrict dealings lest their own institutions be put into jeopardy.

Without global coordination, there can be a race to the bottom, with countries competing to attract financial institutions on the basis of the laxity of regulation. This crisis illustrates the danger of such adverse competition. Countries should realize that the benefits of a larger financial market may be far outweighed by the costs which their citizens may have to pay, as Iceland illustrates.

Circumstances differ across countries, which suggests that the optimal regulation and regulatory structures might differ. Thus, there are items of regulation which should be national in focus with international coordination where the appropriate scope of regulation is international. The dividing line relates to those issues which require a high degree of reciprocity, particularly those issues where inadequate regulation in one country has large effects on other countries, either because of network effects, because of an induced race to the bottom, or because the regulations are designed to check money laundering, financing of terrorism, and tax secrecy.

The dividing line also depends on the representativeness of regulatory bodies. In existing global regulatory bodies, concerns of developing countries are often unrepresented or under-represented. For instance, the Basel I standards encouraged short-term lending (over long-term lending) by developed country banks to developing countries, exacerbating the volatility of their capital flows. Many are concerned that Basel II has the effect of discriminating against developing countries whose institutions do not have the ability to develop the complicated risk management systems it requires—which, in any case, are now recognized as being totally inadequate.

These regulatory systems have been developed by international institutions with biased governance structures, with the under-representation of developing countries and other emerging markets, and with the over influence of the banks being regulated. Basel II is seen by many developing countries as a prime example.

Capital Market Liberalization

Regulations that affect the flow of capital into and out of a country may be among the most important in determining macroeconomic stability and the scope for policy responses in the event of a crisis. There is growing consensus that capital market liberalization may contribute to economic volatility, especially in developing countries. More broadly, a fully integrated global financial system may be subject to more volatility than one with "circuit breakers," such as those employed in many regulated securities exchanges. Part of the reason for this is that capital flows, particularly those to developing countries, tend to be pro-cyclical. And yet, there is little evidence that capital market liberalization contributes to economic growth, especially for less-developed countries. A major reason is that the increased volatility associated with liberalization imposes high costs on an economy, including higher risk premiums, that increase financing costs. Another part may be associated with the fact that much cyclical lending finances consumption rather than investment.

Capital Account Management for Development

Developing countries may need to stabilize international financial flows to promote financial and economic stability, to encourage desirable investment and financing arrangements, to enhance policy autonomy, including the maintenance of stable and competitive exchange rates, and to enhance national sovereignty and democracy. Full capital account convertibility, as well as implicit and explicit agreements to forgo intervention in international capital markets, can make such desirable outcomes impossible.

To achieve these objectives, governments should have the space to undertake capital account management techniques as part of their development and risk management strategies. Such techniques have been used successfully in the past. They have included, but are not limited to, prudential management of foreign borrowing, imposing unremunerated reserve requirements, limiting short-term and other volatile flows, limiting foreign equity ownership of certain financial and other activities, and so on. It is imperative for the success of development strategies that countries undertake dynamic capital account management by having the flexibility to both tighten and loosen controls as and when necessary.

Capital Market Interventions During Crises

Governments have a variety of policy tools to help stabilize financial flows. In a crisis, when traditional instruments such as interest rates are less effective, they may consider temporary restrictions or longer-term taxes on outflows, as well as quantity restrictions. Particularly in the context of a financial and economic crisis, countries may find it necessary to impose restrictions on capital outflows in order to give them more scope for monetary policy discretion.

To a limited extent, counter-cyclical reserve requirements on capital inflows can act as "speed limits" (or "speed bumps") on international capital movements that have a preventive focus and increase the room for counter-cyclical macroeconomic policies. In a similar vein, greater prudential regulation of banks designed to avoid their own currency mismatches as well as those they finance can be simultaneously used as an important instrument in capital account management. In this area, some countries have gone as far as prohibiting financial institutions from holding currency mismatches in their portfolios or lending in foreign currencies to individuals or firms that do not have revenues in those currencies. Others have chosen to increase capital requirements for those who have currency mismatches.

"Host" versus "home" country regulation (see discussion below) may also allow governments greater scope for imposing such stabilizing and development-oriented regulation.

FINANCIAL MARKET LIBERALIZATION

The framework for financial market liberalization under the Financial Services Agreement of the General Agreement on Trade in Services (GATS) under the WTO and, even more, similar provisions in bilateral trade agreements may restrict the ability of governments to change the regulatory structure in ways which support financial stability, economic growth, and the welfare of vulnerable consumers and investors (see Chapter 4, Appendix).

There is some evidence that, at least in some countries, the entry of foreign banks has done nothing to increase lending in general or to small and medium enterprises in particular but has contributed to the faster unwinding of lending in a crisis. Restrictions of the kind proposed in the following paragraphs may be helpful in addressing this concern. Such restrictions should be imposed broadly, on both domestic and foreign banks, even if such uniform restrictions indirectly have a differential effect on foreign banks.

Problems in the banking system in one country can spread to other countries in which that bank has branches or subsidiaries. Parent banks may restrict the lending of their foreign units, or governments may restrict the use of bailout funds to support lending in foreign countries. The current crisis has shown the need to ensure that "national treatment" means effectively equal treatment for domestic banks and foreign subsidiaries.

In order to ensure adequate funding for domestic lending by foreign banks and that the effective capital underlying such lending is not repatriated (as seems to have occurred in some countries), developing countries may find it desirable to require foreign banks to operate as subsidiaries, rather than as branches, and to closely regulate and monitor the outflow of capital from such institutions.

International Banking Centers and International Tax Cooperation

Well-regulated economies have to be protected from those that are under- or unregulated. The problems of tax competition and regulatory arbitrage are often linked. The lack of transparency and regulatory standards in some countries is harmful to the functioning of national tax systems as well as to the financial stability of others. Tax evasion and inappropriate tax practices are major problems for developed as well as developing countries. Each year, developing and developed countries lose revenues that could be used for the financing of development. It is necessary to strive for a universal no-tolerance policy towards financial centers that provide banking secrecy and facilitate tax evasion.

While particular attention has focused on offshore financial centers in developing countries, so far the principal sources of tax evasion, tax secrecy, money laundering, and regulatory arbitrage have been through onshore tax havens in developed countries' financial centers. Delaware and Nevada, for instance, are two U.S. states that make the establishment of anonymous accounts far easier than almost all international banking centers. Bank secrecy remains an issue in several developed country financial centers. London's light touch regulatory regime has also been a source of much regulatory arbitrage. The biggest money laundering cases involved banks in London, New York, and Zurich. The European Commission has decided to refer four smaller member states to the European Court of Justice over non-implementation of the 2005 anti–money laundering directive, and two large member states have been given a final warning. Moreover, the development of financial centers such as London, Luxembourg, and Dublin has been based partly on tax competition, and some developed countries engage in greater tax incentives, subsidies, and tax competition to attract foreign investment than developing countries can afford.

Ad-hoc and discriminatory targeting of the small international financial centers in developing countries while turning a blind eye to lax rules in developed economies is neither fair nor effective. For instance, while many developing country financial centers have several bilateral tax information agreements, the advanced economies do not reciprocate. It is important to move away from bilateral to multilateral agreements.

The determinants of standards and whether particular countries are in violation of those standards must be conducted through a multilateral process in which developing and developed countries have adequate representation. The current dominance of an organization of the advanced industrial countries in this area should be viewed as unacceptable.

The matter would be best handled through multilateral agreements on issues of tax secrecy, which have reciprocity and are enforceable by international courts. The major financial centers should sign up for these agreements first and then urge others to follow, with the threat that those who do not choose to do so will not be allowed to have links with those financial centers that have accepted the conditions of the agreement. Under these agreements, "rogue centers" should be ring-fenced from the rest of the international financial system, but this would be done in an objective manner that could include rich as well as poor countries.

The current system of one rule for the rich and a tougher rule for the poor and the preservation of centers and practices in developed countries that are not permitted in developing countries is patently inequitable. This is why focus should be on the removal of tax secrecy that facilitates tax evasion and highlighting tax avoidance practices. For responsible small states that accept multilateral agreements proposed to eliminate tax secrecy, exporting high-value services that are found in international financial centers is a viable development strategy that has, in fact, been promoted by international financial institutions over the past two decades.

Institutional arrangements for improving harmonization and cooperation on tax matters need to be strengthened. Building on Paragraph 16 of the Financing for Development Doha Declaration of December 2008, the UN Committee of Experts on International Cooperation in Tax Matters, which is part of the UN Economic and Social Council (ECOSOC) system, should be "upgraded" into an intergovernmental body, such as a (functional) commission, to strengthen its ability to enhance international cooperation in this area. It should work to ensure that all countries commit themselves to the voluntary automatic exchange of information that would help root out tax evasion and corruption and also the repatriation of illegal funds. The IMF and other bodies could also have consultative status with the new intergovernmental body.

An International Tax Compact should be instituted that would complement existing initiatives and programs, strengthen the voice and participation of developing countries in ongoing processes, and provide more coordinated support for national tax systems in developing countries. Development cooperation needs to support domestic resource mobilization of developing countries challenged not only by tax evasion and avoidance due to weak domestic tax systems but also the existence of onshore and offshore financial centers facilitating tax evasion. The international community is encouraged to start a dialogue on how to tackle these problems within the framework of an international tax compact.

Of equal concern to developing countries as tax evasion and avoidance is corruption and money laundering, which not only deprive countries of needed resources but also undermine democratic governance. Bank secrecy facilitates this corruption.

Home Versus Host Country Regulation

The trend in financial regulation and supervision, under the auspices of the Bank for International Settlements' attempts to deal with cross-border settlement risk, has been toward home country responsibility. This trend needs to be reversed. Indeed, since host countries are still responsible for the functioning of their real and financial sectors, they can only fulfill that responsibility with effective over-sight over all financial institutions operating within their country. This entails host country supervision and almost surely the require-ment that foreign banks operating in a country establish subsidiaries rather than branches.

Strengthening host country regulation, introducing counter-cyclical capital charges and provisions, redefining the boundary of regulation to be more comprehensive while promoting diversity are all under the remit of domestic regulation—and permitted as part of supervisory discretion under Basel II.

Cross-Border Bankruptcy

The current crisis has illustrated the special problems posed by cross-border bankruptcies. In some cases, citizens of a country have been forced to bear the costs of insuring depositors from other countries. In other cases, worries about the consequences of a default on citizens abroad may have provided part of the rationale for massive govern-ment bailouts and part of the justification for why an institution is too big to fail or to be financially resolved.

FINANCIAL POLICY

Going Beyond Financial Regulation

Ensuring a well-functioning financial market requires, as already noted, more than just financial sector regulation. Financial policies can play an important role in ensuring access to finance, especially for long-term investment and for underserved communities.

Policies outside the financial sector can also play an important role in affecting the behavior of the financial sector but can take on special importance within the financial sector. Examples include competition policy, bankruptcy procedures (financial restructuring), and corporate governance. Failures in any of these areas can have profound systemic effects.

Lending and Public Banking to Promote Development

The objective of financial policy is not only to regulate institutions and the financial system in a prudential manner but also to ensure that the financial sector can live up to its potential positive contribution to society, including ensuring access to credit for all and the provision of credit for long-term development. As already noted, financial sector regulation is a key instrument of financial policy. But there are other instruments which countries, especially developing countries, should consider in order to ensure that the objectives of a good financial system are attained.

In the past, many financial institutions engaged in discrimination in lending to groups or sectors with particular risk characteristics. In the U.S. mortgage market this is known as "redlining." As a result, certain sectors of the economy may not have sufficient access to credit.

Financial institutions have also tended to focus on short-term lending, which is thought to have lower risk than long-term development financing. Financial sector policy in general and, on occasion, regulatory policy can play important roles in filling these lacunae in private institutions' lending practices.

In many countries, government institutions have played an important role in the provision of credit to underserved sectors and segments of society and in promoting development. Development banks have played an important role in the successful financing of development of several countries. Even in advanced industrial countries, these institutions have provided mortgages and credit to small and medium-sized enterprises and to the agricultural sector, financed exports, and provided student loans. Public financial institutions have sometimes done a far better job at providing financial products that mitigate critical risks facing ordinary citizens at lower transaction costs than the private sector. These include public lending programs to finance educational expenses, which have been far more efficient than private lending and have avoided the corruption and abuses that have marked private lending. In many countries, including the U.S., the government has had to introduce special programs to ensure adequate credit access for small and medium-sized enterprises (e.g., partial guarantees, as under the Small Business Administration loan programs). In many successful developing countries, development banks have played an important role at particular stages of their development.

While there has been a presumption that a fully private banking sector is the best system to ensure the most productive and efficient provision of liquidity and management of risk, recent crises have shown another problem with private sector lending—it can be highly cyclical, exacerbating economic fluctuations. In addition, the experience of various developing countries suggests reasons to support a much more substantial role for publicly owned banks and financial institutions. A public bank can substantially realign incentives driving bank managers.

Further, by making the inherent and incessant profit motive subordinate to social objectives, it allows the financial system to exploit the potential for cross-subsidization and to direct credit—even if the bank incurs higher costs—to targeted sectors and disadvantaged sections of society. Given that a significant characteristic of those in poverty is limited access to finance, public banking can thereby facilitate financial inclusion. In the experience of several successful development strategies, public banking has allowed for the mobilization of technical and scientific talent to deliver both credit and technical support to agriculture and the small-scale industrial sectors that have the most direct effect on job creation and poverty reduction.

The current crisis has also highlighted problems associated with pervasive exploitation in the context of mortgages, lending to the poor, and student loans. Given the record of abusive lending to poor individuals, governments may need to consider whether regulatory mechanisms suffice or whether direct lending programs through public sector banks is a better option to reduce abusive practices.

Nevertheless, there is always a danger that public banks may have their portfolios manipulated for political rather than social reasons, and the record of public banks has been spotty. However, some recent experiences of public development banks, with better and more transparent governance structures, are encouraging.

Public and private banks have to coexist in a sustainable financial system. The Keynesian idea that government takes on those tasks the private sector is not able to carry out more efficiently, or where the risks of market failure are too high (including the risk of exploitation), may be one principle in establishing sustainable, developmental, and inclusive banking sectors.

In some banking systems, a large proportion of bank assets are loans to government in the form of holdings of government bonds. Banks that do so are failing to fulfill the critical social function of banks of providing credit to enterprises. This will almost inevitably impair growth and development. Governments should be encouraged to explore various mechanisms by which the banking system could be used to facilitate productive activity. One arrangement, for example, may be for the government to accept savings directly through a network of post offices to reduce the spread between the bank deposit rate and interest charged by banks for government paper and, in doing so, induce banks to look for other ways to enhance the profitability of expanding their lending to productive enterprises.

4

INTERNATIONAL INSTITUTIONS

THE NEED FOR NEW GLOBAL ECONOMIC GOVERNANCE

The inadequacy of the response of international financial institutions to the global financial crisis and their failure to take effective actions to prevent the crisis have demonstrated the urgency of reforming existing international institutions. Such a review needs to include an appraisal of the mandates of these institutions and their governance. Attention also needs to be paid to the policies and philosophies underlying their operations.

There is a need to provide more effective voice and representation for developing countries, which now represent a much larger proportion of world economic activity than in 1944, when the World Bank and the IMF were created. Developing countries, as a group, also have a direct interest in a more equitable global governance system. Above all, it is imperative that reform of the existing institutions should reestablish their credibility as truly international institutions contributing to growth with equity and stability for all countries.

There currently is a unique opportunity to bring forward global economic governance reforms. The current financial and economic crisis not only has made clear the deficiency of existing institutional arrangements but also clearly calls for enhanced cooperation and coordination to deal with it.

Our analysis suggests that not only is there a need for substantial reforms in existing institutions, but that in addition there is also a need to create a new institution, a Global Economic Coordination Council (GECC), supported by an International Panel of Experts. While we understand the concern about the proliferation of international institutions and the hesitancy to create any additional bodies, the need for such a GECC is compelling and spelled out in greater detail below.

Not only did the existing international institutions and institutional arrangements fail to take the actions that might have prevented the current crisis from developing, some institutions even promoted policies that are now recognized to have contributed to the creation and amplification of the crisis and to its rapid spread from the U.S., where it originated, to other countries around the world. Without substantial reform of these institutions (that entails more than a change in name), it will be difficult to ensure financial stability.

The current crisis reflects problems that go beyond the conduct of monetary policy and regulation of the financial sector. It has made clear that globalization of trade and finance calls for enhanced global cooperation and global regulation, as previous chapters have forcefully pointed out.

But the current economic and financial crisis is not the only problem facing the world today. The international community is confronted with multiple, interrelated threats of unprecedented scope besides the collapse of the global financial system and the worldwide economic downturn. The economic crisis followed upon the food and energy crises, which also imposed a high toll on many developing countries. These crises, as well as the growing divide between poor and rich within and between countries and the risk of systemic climate change, are all interconnected global challenges that threaten to unravel the fragile state of globalization.

Global economic integration ("economic globalization") has outpaced the development of the appropriate political institutions and arrangements for governance of the global economic system. Economic globalization means that actions that occur in one country have effects on others. There is a need for global collective action to address not only these issues of global "externalities" but also the provision of global public goods. Among the global public goods are the stability of the global economic system and fair trading rules.

In short, strong global collective action is needed in order to pursue joint goals, particularly the adequate and appropriate provision of global and regional public goods and the broader objectives agreed to in the UN Summits and Conferences of the past two decades. By definition, without coordination, countries do not have sufficient incentives to invest in global and regional public goods (e.g., economic, financial, and ecosystem stability).

The same is true for common social objectives, such as combating poverty. To achieve the goal of sustainable development, stronger collective action is needed in a number of inter-related areas. With the adoption of the Millennium Development Goals, the international community reiterated its commitment to the overarching goal of eradicating poverty. Joint approaches have been agreed upon, and many countries have developed a joint understanding on the relevant financing needs and the respective burden sharing. However, commitments have to be monitored and implemented.

Among the most important of the global public goods is the preservation of the environment. The atmosphere had appeared to have an unlimited ability to absorb greenhouse gas emissions. We now know that is not true and the continuation of emissions at current levels puts the entire planet at risk. Preventing global warming and climate change is a quintessential global public good. The international community thus faces a collective action problem in that there is a need for an international set of rules and incentives that will ensure international cooperation in preserving the self-sustaining nature of the earth's atmosphere.

While the financial crisis has brought to the fore severe structural lacunae in the existing global economic governance structure, in particular the lack of incentives for global collective action (e.g., with regard to the provision of global and regional public goods and poverty reduction) and the failure of the institutional framework to ensure the consistency—or, in UN terminology, coherence—of global policy making, many of the problems have long been apparent. There is a pressing need for a substantial improvement in the coordination of global economic policy. There is also clearly an urgent need to reform the international monetary and financial system to ensure that it is more inclusive and equitable and to thus enable more effective and credible global economic governance.

Already, some developed countries, such as the United Kingdom and France, and many developing countries, such as those in the Commonwealth, have called for an international conference to redesign the system of international economic governance into a new post–Bretton Woods system in order to ensure accountability and transparency in international economic policy making and to overcome existing systemic weaknesses. We agree that there is a compelling need for major reforms, and we hope this report will provide some guidance in any such endeavor. Meanwhile, this chapter focuses on one important initiative, the creation of the GECC, as well as the necessary reforms in existing international institutions. The next chapter discusses some further innovations in the global international architecture that we believe are necessary for sustained global stability and growth.

This chapter is divided into five sections and an appendix. The first discusses briefly the international system of economic governance; the second, the proposal for the creation of a Global Economic Coordination Council; the third, needed reforms in existing international financial institutions; the fourth, international aid; and the fifth, the global system for trade and investment.

THE EXISTING SYSTEM

The existing system of international economic governance has relied on two basic principles: specialization and coordination. A set of global institutions—specialized agencies—were created, each with a mandate to deal with a specific and limited set of issues. The first such economic institutions were the specialized agencies within the UN system, the World Bank and the International Monetary Fund. A third agency called for in the Havana Charter, the International Trade Organization (ITO), was to deal with commercial policy, employment policy coordination, and the position of developing countries but was never approved. Only the General Agreement on Tariffs and Trade (GATT) survived, and it provided, more than three decades later, the basis for the World Trade Organization (WTO), which is not formally part of the UN system. These three post-war international economic

institutions—the World Bank, IMF, and GATT/WTO—were expected
to work in a complementary fashion to promote sustained economic
recovery and growth, full employment, and thus economic welfare, as
well as reconstruction and development of economic capacities and
capabilities. They were complemented by other agencies of the UN
system, which include both the strictly specialized agencies with their
own governance structures (International Labour Organization (ILO),
Food and Agriculture Organization (FAO), UN Educational, Scientific, and Cultural Organization (UNESCO), World Health Organization (WHO), and others) as well as the UN funds and programs (such
as the UN Development Programme (UNDP), UN Environment Programme (UNEP), and UN Children's Fund (UNICEF)).

The overall coordination of UN activities concerned with economic,
social, and ecological affairs, including the specialized agencies, was to
be entrusted to the Economic and Social Council (ECOSOC), one of the
UN system's main organs, in coordination with the General Assembly.
Coherence is not a new concept in the arena of international relations, as
the original UN model provided, in theory, for the coherent design of
policies for the achievement of internationally agreed goals. Although
the system has never worked the way it was originally envisioned, its
internal logic remains compelling; the incomplete arrangements provided support to post-war reconstruction and the Golden Age of
Keynesian-inspired economic growth that existed until the early 1970s.

The underlying challenge to effective global economic governance
originates from the absence, in a world of sovereign states, of an adequate body or bodies as a locus of coordination and accountability
and no way to enforce transparency and elicit compliance. A series of
issues, including cooperation in trade in goods and services, cross-
border environmental goods, cross-border labor policies, payments
and clearing, regulation, contract enforcement, exchange rates, and
other related cross-border matters, have to be addressed through coordinated arrangements which involve negotiated derogations (or
better, sharing) of sovereignty in specific areas.

Neither the G-7 industrialized countries nor the G-20 represents a
sufficiently inclusive global steering group for addressing global systemic challenges. The G-7 has taken a number of initiatives that are

important for developing countries and is engaged in a systematic dialogue particularly with African countries. While the G-20 (which actually has 22 members) is more broadly based, there is still no representation of the remaining 170 countries.

Any future governance format must ensure inclusiveness and adequate representation of developing countries, including least-developed countries (LDCs), promote complementarity and coherence, and establish links between existing and new forums. Thus, although informal groups such as the G-7 and G-20 can play a useful role, they should not be allowed to undermine the functioning of formal institutional arrangements and the discharge of their respective mandates. This inclusive response will require the participation and the involvement of the entire international community. Apart from the G-7, G-8, or G-20, it must encompass representatives of the entire G-192.

The United Nations is the most legitimate forum for addressing the pressing needs of global collective action facing the world today. It can, for instance, play a central role in achieving greater coherence among different actors. Given the specific institutional purposes of the IMF, the World Bank, and other international institutions, there is a need for better coordination and political accountability and for a forum for consensus building to broaden and guide their policy agendas. An overarching theme of the UN Financing for Development (FfD) conference and the resulting Monterrey Consensus was the need to enhance the coherence and consistency of the international monetary, financial, and trading systems to ensure that they support the internationally agreed upon development goals, including social and environmental sustainability.

GLOBAL ECONOMIC COORDINATION COUNCIL

The variety of international institutions and organizations with specific mandates requires an overarching, inclusive body with an integrated view of the economic problems confronting the world and the adequacy of existing institutional arrangements and institutions, including their mandates, policies, instruments, and governance for addressing the economic challenges facing the world today. A globally representative forum, which we call the Global Economic Coordination Council, that addresses areas of concern in the functioning of the global economic system in a comprehensive and sustainable way must be created.

International Panel of Experts

As an immediate step, an International Panel of Experts tasked with the assessment and monitoring of both short-term and long-term systemic risks in the global economy should be established. The panel could serve as an internationally recognized source of expertise in support of better coherence and effectiveness in the global governance system, fostering dialogue between policy makers, the academic world, international organizations, and recognized social movements. The panel should analyze systemic risks in relation to the global economy, their root causes, and their implications for human development. It should establish criteria for the identification of systemic risks and issue recommendations as to preventive measures and sound economic policy making. The panel could thereby also play an important "early-warning function," the need for which has been noted by the G-20 and others. The panel would also identify lacunae and deficiencies in the current global economic system, especially the system of global economic governance, and make suggestions for their remediation. It might, for instance, flesh out some of the proposals in Chapter 5 of this report for the global reserve system, for new mechanisms for better risk bearing, and for alternative proposals for sovereign debt restructuring and dealing with the problems posed by cross-border defaults.

While its analysis would focus on economic issues, it would also take into account the social and ecological dimensions of economic trends and policies and analyze their long-term developmental implications, as well as identify obstacles to economic systems achieving developmental, social, and environmental goals. It should therefore adopt a multidisciplinary and long-term approach to observed economic change.

The panel should be made up of experts from all continents: OECD, emerging, and developing countries. It would not rely on its own research but pool the global knowledge and resources of a large number of acknowledged experts. Such Expert Panels have proven invaluable in other areas of the functioning of the international community where there is a need for expertise to support the political process. Notable examples include the Intergovernmental Panel on Climate Change (IPCC), which has played a critical role in the evolution of global climate change policy, and the scientific panel that led to the Montreal Convention.

The Mandate and Governance of the Global Economic
Coordination Council

In the longer-term, a Global Economic Coordination Council should be established at a level equivalent to the UN General Assembly and the Security Council. Its mandate would be to assess developments and provide leadership in addressing economic issues that require global action while taking into account social and ecological factors. Based on this mandate it would promote development, seek consistency of policy goals and policies of major international organizations, and support consensus building among governments on efficient and effective solutions for global economic, social, and environmental issues. Its work would go beyond simply the coordination of existing institutions. With the support of the Panel of Experts, the GECC could also promote accountability of all international economic organizations, identify gaps that need to be filled to ensure the efficient operation of the global economic and financial system, and make proposals to the international community for remedying deficiencies in the current system.

The Council would have a mandate over the UN system in the economic, social, and environmental fields, which include the Bretton Woods Institutions (BWIs) and should include the WTO by bringing it formally into the UN system, and not only over the UN and its Funds and Programs, as has been characteristic of ECOSOC (which will thus continue exercising its traditional functions). Representation could be based on a constituency system designed to ensure that all continents and all major economies are represented. At the same time, its size should be guided by the fact that the Council must remain small enough for effective discussion and decision-making. In addition, active participation by and consultation with other important institutions, such as the World Bank, IMF, ILO, WTO, and of course the UN Secretariat, would be crucial.

BRETTON WOODS INSTITUTIONS AND REGIONAL DEVELOPMENT BANKS

The IMF and the Multilateral and Regional Development Banks continue to have a very important role in the international economic financial architecture. The mandate of the IMF is to assure global financial and economic stability. It has been expected to survey the economic performance of its member countries, alert them to economic dangers, and provide policy advice and financing to members facing balance of payments difficulties in addition to helping developing nations achieve macroeconomic stability and support employment. While by its own admission the IMF did not perform as well as one might have hoped in identifying systemic vulnerabilities or in anticipating the present crisis, the G-20 has placed special responsibilities on the IMF for helping developing countries respond to the crisis. At the same time, the G-20 has noted deficiencies in existing governance. For the IMF to be fully effective, both in addressing the crisis in the short run and in promoting growth and stability in the long run, there have to be substantial reforms, not only in governance but also in the policies that it has traditionally espoused.

The World Bank and regional development banks are supposed to have a key role in supporting the developing countries, in enhancing their growth and stability and their efforts at reducing poverty. To achieve their objectives they provide concessional loans and grants to developing countries, as well as technical assistance. Within their mandate of poverty reduction and the promotion of sustainable development and inclusive growth, they should play a counter-cyclical role in tackling the crisis. The Multilateral Development Banks (MDBs) have recently revised their policy approach, moving away from earlier market-fundamentalist approaches, starting with debt relief for Heavily Indebted Poor Countries (HIPCs) and the adoption of new poverty alleviation strategies.

The severe shortcomings in the mandate, policies, resources, and governance of these institutions have impaired their ability to take adequate actions to prevent and respond to the crisis and have also had a negative impact on their mandate to promote sustainable development. The ability of the IMF to safeguard the stability of the global economy has been undermined by the vastly greater resources and volatility of globally integrated private financial institutions. Uncoordinated national policy responses have made the task it faces all the more difficult.

The effectiveness and credibility of the Bretton Woods Institutions have been adversely affected by deficiencies in governance (including their skewed voting structures and non-democratic processes of choosing their heads), the checkered record of their forecasting, policy, and other recommendations, including the onerous conditionalities they have imposed on borrowing countries and their tendency to proffer pro-cyclical rather than counter-cyclical policy advice. Major reforms are thus necessary.

There is a global consensus behind recommendations to provide substantial amounts of capital to developing countries that have been the victims of a crisis in the developed world. On the other hand, the means to achieve those capital flows to the developing world have been controversial. The severe conditionalities imposed in the past have in many cases been counterproductive. As noted in Chapter 2, this and other concerns about IMF governance and past performance have led both borrowers and lenders to become reluctant to utilize the IMF.

Surveillance

There is a need for independent and evenhanded macroeconomic surveillance. The IMF has not implemented its mandate consistently and evenhandedly. For example, in recent decades, it has largely ignored its mandate to sustain growth and employment and has focused almost exclusively on curbing inflation. It has also promoted financial, including capital account, liberalization, although its Articles of Agreement clearly allow governments to use capital controls. Before the current crisis, the IMF also failed to provide early warnings—unlike the UN system in various publications such as the *World Economic Situation and Prospects* and the *Trade and Development Report.*

Surveillance should pay special attention to those countries and sectors that are systemically important, including the financial sectors in the U.S. and Europe. It should also address the adequacy of the "circuit breakers" that might prevent the contagion of a problem in one country from spreading to another.

The GECC and the International Panel of Experts can play an important role in monitoring the adequacy of surveillance and whether these deficiencies have been adequately addressed.

Public Goods and the Multilateral Development Banks

Developing countries' actions in support of the provision of global and regional public goods need additional funding if other developmental objectives are not to be compromised. The provision of global and regional public goods should thus be an important part of development institutions' work and mandates. In some areas, such as combating climate change, the different dimensions associated with the provision of global public goods needs to be assessed, including the implications for the respective mandates of the UN Framework Convention on Climate Change (UNFCCC) and the World Bank.

Given the critical nature of climate change, support for developing country efforts at reducing emissions is of special importance. The architecture for financing climate change–related expenditures will be reviewed in the course of the UN climate negotiations. From a development perspective, the key issue is that climate-related tasks in the developing countries are considered as an integral part of a sustainable development agenda and that all partners act accordingly. To that end, the full set of existing development instruments, procedures, and institutions must be used and further developed. Multilateral climate financing must come under the authority of the UNFCCC and serve to meet its climate change mitigation and adaptation objectives.

GOVERNANCE

There is a growing international consensus in support of reform of the governance, accountability, and transparency in the International Financial Institutions (IFIs). The governance reforms have to be based on a joint understanding of the respective mandates and a common understanding of the strategic directions of the respective institutions. The inconsistency between the economic and financial weight of developing countries in the world economy and their role as recipients of IMF and World Bank funds, on the one hand, and their representation in these institutions, on the other, is one of the factors behind the loss of legitimacy and relevance of those organizations in addressing systemic issues. Better voice and representation of developing countries in IFIs must therefore be high on the agenda. Governance reform must strengthen, in particular, the weight of low-income countries.

The participation of developing countries is essential if there is to be an adequate provision of global and regional public goods, such as climate protection and financial stability. Accordingly, these agendas can only be successfully realized if the developing country perspective is appropriately reflected in global decision-making.

International Monetary Fund Governance Reform

To strengthen the effectiveness and legitimacy of the IMF, its governance must be enhanced to ensure that it fully reflects changes in the world economy. Emerging and developing economies, including the poorest, should have greater voice and representation. On this basis, major reforms in the governance of this institution, including giving greater voice to developing countries and greater transparency, have to be accelerated. The Report of the Committee of Eminent Persons on IMF Governance Reform, chaired by Trevor Manuel, contains interesting recommendations in this regard. The IMF (and other international institutions) should aspire to the highest standards of transparency and consider the introduction of the kinds of principles embodied in the Freedom of Information Acts and Right to Know laws that have been adopted by democracies throughout the world.

The decisions for broader reform taken by the Board of Governors of the IMF at its Annual Meetings in Singapore in 2006 and in Washington in 2008 have resulted in modest progress. Quota reform has only been made on an ad hoc basis, first in 2006 for a small group of emerging market countries and in April 2008 for the larger membership, leading to marginal changes that failed to shift significantly the balance of power between developed and developing countries. The April 2008 decision by the Board of Governors to adopt a new quota formula is not sufficient to address the problems in governance. In fact, the new formula actually shifts voting weight to industrial countries at the expense of middle- and low-income ones, with the modest progress achieved due to voluntary forgoing of votes by major industrial countries and ad hoc decisions. Therefore, a step towards more inclusiveness and representative governance at the IMF would require an improved quota formula and/or alternative procedural reforms.

Strengthening the voting weight of low-income countries can be done by increasing quotas or by further increasing the share of basic votes. When the IMF was established in 1944, basic votes were set at 250 votes for each member and represented 11.3% of total voting power when it had 44 members. However, as a result of the increase in quotas that has occurred over the years, the share of basic votes has fallen considerably and reached its lowest level of 2.1% of total voting power for 184 members in the mid-2000s! The April 2008 decision taken by the IMF Board of Governors to reverse this trend by tripling basic votes only increased the total share of basic votes to 5.5% of current voting power, which falls far short of restoring the share let alone the weight of basic votes.

The application of double majority voting to a broader set of decisions could also compensate for voting imbalances at the IMF. At present, a double majority—85% of voting power and a 60% majority of members—is required to amend the Articles of Agreement. Double majority voting (e.g., shares and chairs) should be extended to the selection of the Managing Director and the chair of the IMF Committee, as well as for key policy decisions and approval of access to lending operations. At the same time, the reform must consider eliminating effective veto powers over decisions to amend the Articles of Agreement. These changes could help strengthen the sense of ownership in the IMF by requiring a significant majority of members to support key decisions that determine the direction of the organization. Consideration should be given to alternative forms of double majority (e.g., developed and developing countries).

International Bank for Reconstruction and Development Governance Reform

Some of the basic principles for IMF governance reform would apply to reforming other international financial institutions, such as the World Bank. However, the Bank's specific mandate as a development bank is distinct from the IMF, and its governance should reflect this difference. Hence, in determining the participation rights of its members, distinct World Bank governance arrangements would be needed.

The first stage of the World Bank's voice reform should be implemented rapidly. The doubling of basic votes and a third African seat on the Board will increase the influence of developing countries. The second stage, focusing on a reform of quotas, should be accelerated and completed by the Spring Meetings in 2010. With regard to the quota reform, three criteria should be taken into account for allocating votes: the member states' economic weight, their contribution to the development mandate of the World Bank (for example, measured in terms of contributions to International Development Association [IDA] and trust funds), and the significance of borrowing levels from the Bank. The two latter criteria would reward member states for being closely connected with the Bank.

Against the background of the challenges ahead, such as the financial crisis and climate change, the second stage of the reform process should start with an in-depth debate on the Bank's mandate and its strategic directions. The World Bank Group already has different "arms," such as IDA and the International Bank for Reconstruction and Development (IBRD), with their own governance structures. New fields, or traditional areas becoming a new focus of support, such as the increasing role of the Bank in the area of global and regional public goods or aid for trade, might also require new governance structures as well as new ways of interacting with other global institutions.

Common Issues

Other important governance reforms include reforms in the way that the head of the institution and the most senior officers are chosen and conflict of interest reforms ("revolving doors") consistent with the best practices of democratic governance. Within the IMF and the World Bank there should be a merit-based, transparent process for the selection of the senior management. Conventions associated with the choice of the leaders of the World Bank and the IMF make little sense in the 21st century.

Given the wide impact of IMF programs and the steady expansion of its operations into the areas of development and poverty alleviation, it does not seem appropriate that the IMF should just reflect the views of representatives from finance ministries and central banks. The views of development and planning ministries should be better integrated. The same principle should be applied to the World Bank, as it has along the way added new tasks to its mandate, in particular in the area of global and regional public goods such as health and environmental policy. Doing so will promote coherence between the policies of national governments and those of the international institutions.

OTHER INTERNATIONAL FINANCIAL BODIES

The governance of global financial regulation remains a question of concern. While national regulatory authorities have the ability and mandate to protect the vulnerable within their borders, there is a difficulty in extending this mission across borders. The present crisis has shown how deficient regulation on the part of one country can have adverse effects on others. Unless effective coordination in global financial regulation is achieved, as we noted in Chapter 3, there is the risk of fragmentation of the global financial system, as each country will seek to protect itself from toxic products and practices originating from abroad. (While much of what is to be done at the international level will be difficult to achieve in the short-term, there is a great deal that can be done at the domestic level without prior international agreement. The necessary reforms are discussed at length in Chapter 3.)

Existing institutional arrangements have obviously proven ineffective for reasons that will be explained more fully below. Again, the international community faces the difficult choice between reforming existing institutions and creating new institutions. Reform of existing institutions may be difficult, for the staff of those institutions are often wedded to the economic philosophies that have contributed so much to the crisis. Moreover, it has proven difficult, at best, to reform existing institutions sufficiently to create confidence in them, especially within developing countries. It is therefore imperative that there should be consideration of a new Global Financial Authority to coordinate financial regulation in general and to establish and/or coordinate global rules in certain areas, such as regarding money laundering and tax secrecy. (Chapter 3 discusses the role that the UN Committee of Experts on International Cooperation in Tax Matters should play in these efforts.)

The FSF was created in the aftermath of the 1997–1998 financial crisis in order to promote international financial stability, improve the functioning of financial markets, reduce the tendency for financial shocks to propagate from country to country, and enhance the institutional framework to support global financial stability. It is now apparent that the reforms that it has proposed have not been sufficient to avoid major global financial instability. These failures imply that there will need to be substantial reform if there is to be confidence that it will fulfill its mandate. In April 2009, the Financial Stability Forum (FSF) was reestablished as the Financial Stability

Board (FSB). Chapter 3 explains the need for robust regulations—a marked departure from the stance of the FSF. Making marginal changes to the regulatory structure would neither ameliorate the current situation nor be effective in preventing future crises.

Deeper reforms in the FSB must, accordingly, address deficiencies in its governance, mandate, and economic perspectives. The initial move to strengthen and reform the FSF (now the FSB), as agreed at the April 2009 G-20 Summit, should only be an initial step toward establishing much more representative, appropriate, and effective financial regulation at both national and international levels. The proposed widening of the membership is, for instance, necessary if there is to be international confidence in the FSB's effectiveness and balance, but governance and participation reforms have not gone far enough.

In particular, the FSB and all other standard-setting institutions must become more representative and accountable to adequately reflect the views of and the conditions in developing countries. Most developing countries are not represented in today's standard-setting institutions. The Basel Committee of the Bank for International Settlements (BIS) and the FSF/FSB set important global economic standards in areas such as data dissemination, bank supervision, financial regulation, and corporate governance. While the original intention of the Basel Committee was to provide regulations for large internationally active banks, the Committee's regulatory proposals have been generally adopted by most countries. As a result, the inadequate representation of developing countries in these ad hoc bodies has made their analysis and recommendations incomplete and biased in crucial aspects. Inattention to the fact that countries are at different stages of economic development with varying financial and institutional capacities poses a challenge for global acceptance of standards and codes developed by these non-inclusive bodies. This dilemma is a major obstacle to universal and effective implementation. While standard setters liaise with developing and transition economies from time to time, consultations do not substitute for participating in the decision-making.

The task of ensuring coherence in regulatory principles among national authorities must be undertaken by international standard-setting bodies, such as the U.S. Financial Accounting Standards Board (FASB), supported by an accountable Secretariat with access to a diversity of viewpoints. For the FSB to take on this role as a global authority in identifying systemic risk for the financial system, it would require an international capability that goes beyond that of the FSB and the BIS. International financial regulation will require coordination beyond central banks (the major constituency of the BIS) and must include securities and corporate regulators as well as accounting standards among its key priorities.

By the same token, if the FSB is to become the main instrument for the formulation of reforms of the global financial system, it must do a better job in taking into consideration the distinctive aspects of developing country economies, how regulations in developed countries may affect the economies of the developing countries, and the importance of financial stability for economic development. But it should also be cognizant of how financial sector regulation and development can affect the growth of developing countries. Previous regulatory structures (Basel I and Basel II), in addition to all of their other flaws and inadequacies, may have (perhaps unintentionally) discriminated against developing countries.

The challenge is to create globally representative institutions that are cognizant of the concerns of the advanced industrial countries, emerging markets, and developing countries. Even if it is not easy to change institutional cultures, more inclusive and appropriate representation in the BIS and FSB would result not only in a fairer system but also in better regulation leading to a more stable global financial system with welfare-enhancing effects for all. It would be less dominated by those who have benefited from current arrangements, with greater voice from those countries that have not benefited. But as Chapter 3 has pointed out, self-regulation cannot work, and regulation dominated by those from the sector being regulated should be viewed as, at best, problematic. Increased international public oversight in the governance of the international financial system requires that critical standard-setting activities are, at a minimum, reported to an intergovernmental body for coordination, such as the GECC described earlier.

The lack of accountability of important, private standard-setting bodies is an additional area of concern. Private entities such as the International Accounting Standards Board (IASB) and the International Organization of Securities Commissions (IOSCO) develop, for instance, standards for cross-border regulation that have systemic impacts on the international financial system, yet they are exempt from any political accountability. Increased international public oversight of governance of the international financial system requires that critical standard-setting activities, at a minimum, be reported to an intergovernmental body for approval. This is particularly important in light of the greater interconnectedness among financial market segments. Global banks have increasingly expanded their operations into securities markets and own or control brokerage and security firms.

INTERNATIONAL LENDING AND OFFICIAL DEVELOPMENT ASSISTANCE

There is an urgent need for donors to fulfill their existing bilateral and multilateral Official Development Assistance (ODA) commitments. Developed countries must make a renewed effort to meet the commitments made in the UN Millennium Declaration, the Monterrey Consensus, the 2005 Global Summit, and the Doha Declaration by 2015. The consequences of a failure to do so have been described elsewhere in this report.

Additional Funding for Developing Countries Needed

Funding is required to contain the negative impact of the crisis on developing countries as well as to offset the distortions of the level playing field created by some of the massive stimulus and bailout programs of the advanced industrial countries, including large subsidies to financial institutions and corporations and extensive guarantees. (See the discussion in Chapter 2.)

Aid Effectiveness

The processes for achieving aid effectiveness need significant enhancement. The 2002 Monterrey Consensus asserted that "effective partnerships among donors and recipients are based on the recognition of national leadership and ownership of development plans and, within that framework, sound policies and good governance at all levels, are necessary to ensure ODA effectiveness." The 2005 Paris Declaration on Aid Effectiveness sought to operationalize these basic principles. Despite commendable early OECD leadership in this area, a more universal body, where all parties share responsibility for progress, can effectively lead in further enhancing aid effectiveness. The Development Cooperation Forum (DCF) of ECOSOC has begun promising work in this area.

Donor conditionalities and the realizing of national ownership of development strategies were the most contentious issues in negotiating the 2008 Accra Agenda for Action, which affirmed that national ownership and effective leadership are unattainable without a reform of conditionality. Achieving national leadership will require a shared understanding of what conditionality is appropriate and mutually acceptable. Aid recipients must meaningfully participate in the agenda setting and operations of multilateral institutions that manage development aid. ODA should not undermine national accountability, democratic processes, parliamentary oversight, or national capacities for designing, negotiating, and implementing development strategies appropriate to domestic conditions.

Ironically, ODA has proven to be the most volatile of foreign flows to many of the poorest countries in the world. Improving the predictability of aid is necessary for aid effectiveness. The international community must make progress to genuinely align aid programs with national priorities.

The use of governance indicators (and more broadly, the Country Policy and Institutional Assessment indicators) for aid allocation and other international cooperation has been greatly discredited. Yet these indicators are currently a critical element in determining access to aid and debt financing for developing countries. They should no longer be used as a basis of aid allocation, as they represent a hidden form of conditionality.

Expansion of Resources by IFIs

Steps must be taken to ensure that the World Bank and the regional development institutions have sufficient financial capabilities, as these institutions must be able to provide counter-cyclical financing. It is necessary to determine whether certain international financial institutions may possibly require a capital increase, which is doubtless the case with the Asian and Inter-American Development Banks. There is also a case for early replenishment of IDA funds, since without such replenishment and/or other form of fund enhancement, many developing countries may be reluctant to take enhanced IDA funding in response to the crisis for fear that there will be insufficient funds available in subsequent years.

In order to be able to react more promptly in future crises, the MDBs' policies and facilities should be reviewed. There could prove to be a need for additional facilities within their respective mandates (including the support for safety net/social protection measures discussed earlier) and the establishment of a fast-track mode of project preparation.

In addition, regional efforts to augment liquidity should be supported. Regional cooperation arrangements can be particularly effective because of a greater recognition of cross-border externalities and greater sensitivities to the distinctive conditions in neighboring countries.

Immediate Expansion of IMF Resources

It is obvious that the IMF's current lending resources are not sufficient to allow it to respond appropriately to the worsening problems in developing countries. To allow the IMF to fulfill its mandate of stabilizing the global economy and to respond to increased members' demands in the current uncertain international environment, the

IMF's position should be strengthened through a very substantial increase in its lending capacity along the lines already decided at the recent London G-20 meeting. This will require reviewing the various options, including the allocation of further special drawing rights (SDRs) already agreed upon, bilateral loans, an expansion of the membership and scale of the New Agreements to Borrow (NAB), and completion of the quota review now scheduled for 2011. The resource increase should go in parallel with decisive progress in long-overdue governance and voice reforms, along the lines discussed earlier.

Debt Sustainability

Several developing countries are facing debt sustainability problems. The new Debt Sustainability Framework recently introduced by the IFIs is meant to be forward looking and prevent debt servicing problems before they arise by limiting a country's debt position. However, the current crisis suggests that there should be a further assessment of MDBs' policies, (both in terms of what is considered to be sustainable debt dynamics and what the appropriate responses are to situations in which the debt dynamics appear unsustainable). In those countries where the crisis is seriously threatening debt sustainability, consideration could be given to debt moratoria and, where appropriate, partial debt cancellation within the framework of a permanent international debt regime (see Chapter 5 for further details). Furthermore, low-income countries in particular need more access to highly concessional funds and grants if they are to meet their essential spending needs and respond in a counter-cyclical way to the crisis without getting back into debt difficulties. The current provisions of the G-20 in this regard are too limited in scope. The various options, such as an early replenishment of IDA funds, should be examined. Also, MDBs and other donors should make every effort to make repayment flexible in response to exogenous shocks. Better systems of risk mitigation and risk sharing (along the lines discussed in Chapter 5) need to be explored and developed.

A New Credit Facility

In order to mobilize additional funds, the creation of a new credit facility is a matter of urgency. The new facility, which has been more fully discussed in Chapter 2, could draw upon financial contributions from all countries. It could leverage any equity funds contributed by borrowing in financial markets. Countries that have accumulated large reserves, including those that are commodity exporters, could use their surpluses to make direct investments in developing countries. It would benefit both developing countries and the world economy if savings from emerging markets could be at least partly transferred to developing country projects. The new credit facility's ability to borrow could be enhanced through guarantees provided by governments, especially those of the advanced industrial countries. Chapter 2 discussed the various uses to which these funds could be put, including investment projects in key sectors, such as agriculture, financing temporary guarantees for trade credit or for the debt of their corporations, forestalling the risk of a run on these corporations. The current financial system does not provide these intermediary services.

Commodities Trade and Compensatory Financing

The volatility of export earnings of countries dependent on primary commodity exports has long been recognized as a key source of instability in the global economic system. Unless they take strong protective measures, these countries not only experience boom-bust cycles but also tend to find themselves in debt distress and in need of additional aid when commodity prices collapse. Developing countries that are dependent on exports of commodities with high price volatility need to establish stabilization funds and to otherwise manage their economies to reduce the extent of the boom-bust cycle, including by restricting borrowing during the boom phase. But, inevitably, such management will be imperfect, and there will be need for compensatory finance. When it is provided, it is important that it be done in ways that do not impose counterproductive conditionalities. The international community, including the IFIs, should explore ways of mitigating the risks from commodity fluctuations, including perhaps by providing loans in which repayments vary with commodity prices.

TRADE AND INVESTMENT

The World Trade Organization (WTO) is the only universal body for setting trade rules and resolving trade disputes. The WTO is the only universal intergovernmental institution which, at the insistence of major industrial countries, does not have an institutional agreement with the UN (i.e., the "Arrangements for Effective Cooperation with other Intergovernmental Organizations—Relations Between the WTO and the United Nations" of 15 November 1995, provides only for informational cooperation), even though it has separately acceded to coherence commitments with the Bretton Woods Institutions. Given its status as a major stakeholder in the UN Financing for Development process, the WTO should be brought into the UN system of global economic governance while maintaining its legal and institutional constituency.

Through the WTO dispute settlement mechanism, small or weak countries have a means to defend themselves against unfair trade practices, but asymmetric legal and other resources, as well as limited developing country participation in drawing up existing rules and regulations, limit the mechanism's potential to promote justice and development. Imbalances in WTO accession practices, trade dispute mechanisms, and negotiation modalities have also placed developing countries and new members at a disadvantage, besides deterring the possibility that it might serve as a model for a similar organization for international finance. All countries acceding to the Principles and Agreements of the WTO should be given membership. There needs to be an end to the current practice of "extortion at the gate." In particular, developing countries seeking membership should not be subjected to conditions that go beyond those to which existing members are subjected. Furthermore, developed countries need to provide developing countries with additional resources for support of adequate legal representation in the dispute settlement mechanism.

The growth of bilateral trade agreements may undermine the multilateral trading system. Indeed, the fragmentation of the global trading system is a major step backwards in creating a system of free international trade. The resulting "Rules of Origin" regime, for instance, undermines the free flow of goods and services across borders, one of the objectives of the multilateral trading system. Developing countries are often put in a more disadvantageous position in these bilateral trade negotiations than they are in multilateral trade negotiations.

Protectionism in the Midst of the Crisis

Reform of rules governing international trade has the potential to stem protectionism and could provide a signal of confidence in a time of crisis. But the current crisis has exposed limits to the effectiveness of these measures shielding the world from protectionism. The WTO should be commended for its work monitoring these protectionist actions in the current crisis.

The global crisis has been marked by precipitous declines in world trade. The dangers of trade contraction represent a far more serious risk to the global economy than in the Great Depression because trade today is so much more important for many economies. Those low-income countries that are heavily dependent on exports will suffer severely from trade contraction, and commodity exporters will suffer doubly as a result of the collapse of many commodity prices.

These inevitable consequences of a global contraction of trade have been augmented by protectionism. Throughout the world, protectionism has increased. In its initial communiqué, the G-20 warned of these dangers, and the members committed themselves not to engage in protectionism. Yet, pressures for protectionism have been difficult to resist.

Trade restrictions, subsidies, guarantees, and domestic restrictions on government procurement contained in some stimulus packages and recovery programs distort world markets. Although international agreements contain the same rules for each country, due to very different economic and social points of departure, seemingly "symmetric" provisions can have markedly asymmetric effects.

For instance, government procurement provisions under the financial stimulus packages sometimes heavily distort competition at the expense of developing countries, since signatories of the WTO plurilateral agreements on government procurement are mainly industrialized countries.

Subsidies, implicit and explicit, can be just as (or even more) distorting to open and fair trade as tariffs. (See the more extensive discussion in Chapter 2.) As has been recognized, subsidies can create an uneven playing field just as tariffs do, but these are even more unfair, since only rich countries can afford subsidies. Firms in developing countries simply can't compete against those in the more developed countries that receive massive assistance from their governments, whether in the form of open subsidies (including bailouts) or less transparent subsidies (guarantees and access to government or central bank lending). While the domestic imperatives that give rise to domestic subsidies are understandable, efforts need to be made to finance additional support to developing countries to mitigate the impact of the crisis as well as of both open and hidden subsidies in order to avoid further distortions.

The WTO should systematically assess the policies conducted by Member States in the framework of their stimulus and recovery packages, giving adequate attention to the consistency of the letter and spirit of WTO agreements, the exigencies of the situation, and the adverse effects, especially on developing countries. We need to avoid at all costs a return to the beggar-thy-neighbor policies that the creation of the WTO was intended to prevent.

In these assessments, attention should be paid both to the "legal" and "illegal" protectionist measures. An example of legal but nonetheless harmful protectionist measures are the domestic procurement provisions in certain stimulus packages, mentioned above. Other examples include the increased use of non-tariff barriers, such as safeguards and dumping duties. It has long been recognized, for instance, that WTO legal criteria for dumping do not accord with standard notions of predatory pricing ("unfair competition") and represent a major exception to WTO principles of non-discrimination: if these standards were applied domestically, a large fraction of domestic firms in many advanced industrial countries would be guilty of dumping. It has also been recognized that these criteria may be, and have been, used discriminatorily against developing countries. Just as beggar-thy-neighbor tariffs can lead to retaliation, so too can non-tariff barriers. There can be retaliation, for instance, by bringing dumping and countervailing duty cases. This would undermine progress in creating an open and fair global trading regime.

At the same time, some developing countries are being subjected to pressure not to raise tariffs, even when existing tariffs are substantially below the bound rates and when raising these tariffs might help stabilize these economies and help them cope with the crisis.

These problems (and the problems discussed in previous chapters on financial market liberalization) highlight deficiencies in existing global rules, e.g. concerning non-tariff barriers, financial market liberalization, and the ability to respond to crises.

In our Preliminary Report released in February 2009, we urged developed countries to unilaterally open up their markets to the goods of the least-developed countries, globalizing and strengthening the Everything but Arms initiative. Further extending that initiative so that even middle-income countries opened up their markets to those countries that were smaller and poorer could be very beneficial to the developing countries and help deal with the economic shock of the crisis.

Reductions in non-tariff barriers could substantially stimulate the global economy. As tariff barriers come down, the importance of non-tariff barriers increases, and some, such as phyto-sanitary conditions, are particularly and differentially harmful to developing countries.

The Doha Round

Recent discussions have often highlighted the importance of the completion of the Doha Round of trade negotiations. However, after the initiation of the Doha Round negotiations, the development thrust has been lost, and whatever the merits of the current proposals, they do not deserve to be called a "development round." Serious studies suggest that the conclusion of the round, regardless of its symbolic value, is unlikely to make much difference for low-income countries and particularly for least-developed countries. An agreement at the existing stage of negotiations could or would be at the cost of its development content without providing any change to international market dynamics in favor of developing countries. It would be especially unfortunate if there were a sense that, having completed the "development round," there would be a return to the unfair kinds of trade negotiations that have marked the past.

The current Doha negotiations on multilateral trade risk descending into a "one size fits all" approach, with narrow focus on market access to all countries, irrespective of their economic circumstances. The round has been increasingly reduced to an endless bargaining session between industrialized countries and emerging markets about market access in industrialized goods. Consequently, as the original spirit of development orientation has faded away, the likely benefits to low-income countries have diminished, and completion of the round has become endangered by deadlocked positions of major WTO members.

What is needed is a renewal of commitment by all countries to the original spirit of Doha, a true development round. Rapid completion of negotiations within that spirit could be of benefit to all countries and help offset the adverse effects on trade of the current recession.

The 2004 ILO Commission on the Social Dimension of Globalization pointed out that developing countries today cannot take advantage of many policies that have been used by industrialized countries in their developmental process. Particularly troubling are provisions in both bilateral and multilateral trade agreements that go beyond trade into intellectual property and investment and which may restrict the ability of developing countries to design appropriate regulatory regimes.

Capital and Financial Market Liberalization

Capital and financial market liberalization, pushed not only by the IMF but also within certain trade agreements, exposed developing countries to more risk and has contributed to the rapid spread of the crisis around the world. In particular, trade-related financial services liberalization has been advanced under the rubric of the WTO's General Agreement on Trade in Services (GATS) Financial Services Agreement with insufficient regard for its consequences either for growth or stability. Externalities exerted by volatility in the financial sector have severe negative effects on all areas of the economy and are an impediment to a stable development path. Chapter 3 and discussions earlier in this chapter emphasized how inadequate regulation in one country may harm others. Unfortunately, while the GATS Financial Services Agreement provides the only significant regulatory framework for international financial services, it was not conceived and negotiated with these broader considerations in mind but rather was driven by sectoral interests. These special interests often do not realize (or care about) the vulnerabilities that these commitments impose on other aspects of their economy or the international economy.

The crisis has brought home the importance of a strong financial market regulatory regime. It has also exposed new risks as international banks reduce lending in developing countries in order to preserve lending at home. Recent research has also called into question whether financial market liberalization enhances economic growth. At least in many instances, there is a tendency for foreign-owned banks to restrict lending to small and medium-sized businesses as they concentrate on lending to government, multinational corporations, and/or large domestic monopolies and oligopolies. Financial market liberalization may bring risk without reward. As Chapter 3 has emphasized, a well-functioning financial system requires regulation, not only to ensure the safety and soundness of banks and stability of the financial system and the economy but also to ensure competition and access to funds and to prevent abusive lending practices.

One of the central arguments for financial market liberalization was that foreign banks (including those from the United States) were better at risk management and credit assessment than domestic banks and thus entry of these banks into a market would improve the competencies of domestic banks. The massive failures of U.S. banks have cast doubt on the validity of that presumption.

Developing countries also need policy frameworks that can enable them to protect themselves from regulatory and macroeconomic failures in systemically significant countries. To achieve this as well as to develop appropriate regulatory policies, for instance of the kind discussed in Chapter 3, policy space is a necessary precondition.

Policy space is restricted not only by a lack of resources but also by multilateral and bilateral agreements and by the conditionalities accompanying assistance. Many bilateral and regional trade agreements contain commitments that restrict the ability of countries to respond to the current crisis with appropriate regulatory, structural, and macroeconomic reforms and support packages. Developing countries have had imposed on them deregulation policies akin to those that are now recognized as having played a role in the onset of the crisis. In addition, they have also faced restrictions on their ability to manage their capital account and financial systems (e.g., as a result of financial and capital market liberalization policies). These policies are placing a heavy burden on many developing countries.

Agreements that restrict a country's ability to revise its regulatory regime—including not only domestic prudential but, crucially, capital account regulations—obviously have to be altered, in light of what has been learned about deficiencies in this crisis. In particular, there is concern that existing agreements under the WTO's Financial Services Agreement might, were they enforced, impede countries from revising their regulatory structures in ways that would promote growth, equity, and stability.

More broadly, all trade agreements need to be reviewed to ensure that they are consistent with the need for an inclusive and comprehensive international regulatory framework which is conducive to crisis prevention and management, counter-cyclical and prudential safeguards, development, and inclusive finance. Commitments and existing multilateral agreements (such as GATS) as well as regional trade agreements, which seek greater liberalization of financial flows and services, need to be critically reviewed in terms of their balance of payments effects, their impacts on macroeconomic stability, and the scope they provide for financial regulation. Macroeconomic stability, an efficient regulatory framework, and functioning institutions are necessary preconditions for liberalization of financial services and the capital account, not vice versa. Strategies and concepts of opening up developing economies need to include appropriate reforms and sequencing. This is of particular importance for small and vulnerable economies with weak institutional capacities. But there has to be a fundamental change in the presumptions that have guided efforts at liberalization. As noted in previous chapters, one of the lessons of the current crisis is that there should be no presumption that *eventually* there should be full liberalization. Rather, even the most advanced industrial countries require strong financial market regulations

CONCLUDING COMMENTS

This crisis has exposed a large number of failings in the system of global economic governance. These failings have left the world unnecessarily exposed to grave risks and less prepared to cope with the current crisis.

Previous chapters have highlighted the need for global collective action arising out of the interdependencies that have resulted from greater economic integration. There is a need for cooperation in the design of the macroeconomic responses and in the global regulatory regime.

As we have repeatedly noted, economic globalization has outpaced the development of adequate global institutions to help manage globalization. When national economies were formed, national institutions were gradually developed to help manage their economies. These include institutions and regulatory frameworks to ensure competition, to protect consumers and investors, to manage bankruptcies, to enforce contracts, and to ensure the stability of the economy. With the increase in cross-border economic activity, the functioning of the world economy will require the creation of institutions and institutional arrangements fulfilling similar functions at the global level. Critics will worry that a wide array of new institutions might result. But these new institutions and institutional arrangements are simply the consequence of the new challenges presented by globalization.

This chapter has highlighted the reforms that are needed in the existing institutions—in how they are governed, their mandates, their instruments and policies, and the economic philosophies that have been the basis of the policies that they have advocated and pursued. In many cases, the developing countries in particular have suffered as a result of the shortcomings of these institutions.

But this chapter has also highlighted the need for the creation of a Global Economic Coordination Council to provide better coherence in the management of the global economy. Such a Council would identify some of the key problems facing the governance of the global economy today.

The next chapter proposes several innovative solutions to a few of the key issues.

APPENDIX: THE DOHA ROUND AND DEVELOPMENT

This appendix discusses several aspects of the Doha Round of trade negotiations as they affect development. As we have noted, the development round, as negotiations have proceeded, has rightly been criticized for having lost much of its original mission of rectifying the imbalances of past trade negotiations and actively promoting the development and well-being of those in the developing world.

Some have argued that an important step forward would be the elimination of all forms of agricultural export subsidies by the end of 2013 (as agreed to during the Hong Kong Ministerial Conference of December 2005). However, the full benefits of such a commitment hinge upon a series of other mandated negotiating objectives being met. It is in the nature of negotiations that early harvest outcomes, based on selected elements of the negotiating modalities—however attractive they may seem—risk reducing the gains that would accrue to developing countries, and may have the effect of making an outcome in areas of crucial relevance to developing countries less likely politically, not more.

This is all the more so because export subsidies do not constitute the bulk of the distorting trade arsenal of developed countries. Developing countries would greatly benefit if other forms of distorting support were substantially reduced in line with the Doha mandate. This means bringing down permitted levels of Overall Trade-Distorting Domestic Support (OTDS) and further limitations to the various "boxes" (AMS, Blue Box, Green Box, and de minimis) as well as effective monitoring in order to prevent big subsidizing developed nations from shifting their domestic programs from one "box" to another. Many of the so-called non–trade distorting subsidies actually do distort trade. These reforms need to be complemented by product-specific disciplines that restrain maximum allowed levels of support by developed countries on a per-product basis. This is an especially important outcome of the round for developing countries, as it improves market conditions for agricultural goods of particular interest to them.

The cotton dispute is a dramatic example of how trade-distorting export subsidies and internal support in the rich, developed economies can undermine income generation and growth prospects in poor countries, affecting their capacity to become players in their own right in the global marketplace and thereby relegating them to dependence on aid or on other kinds of non-binding commitments or concessions over which they have no control.

The fact that distorting cotton subsidies remain in place, in spite of the ruling of the WTO's Appellate Body against them, threatens the credibility of the WTO dispute settlement system.

In the important area of industrial goods, or non-agricultural market access (NAMA), there cannot be full reciprocity in tariff reduction if the asymmetries that have worked historically to the detriment of developing countries are to be addressed. The two goals are simply at odds. Accordingly, special attention needs to be given to the problem of tariff escalation, which restricts the ability of developing countries to move up the value chain.

Furthermore, developed countries should not try to extract additional concessions from developing countries in sectoral negotiations that would negate the principle of less-than-full reciprocity. The Development Round was intended in part to rectify previous imbalances in trade negotiations; demanding full reciprocity would obviously run counter to that goal.

Moreover, an acceptable package must also include binding commitments on Special and Differential Treatment for developing countries through exceptions to and longer transition periods for LDCs to implement their obligations as well as other mechanisms that allow developing countries greater flexibility in coping with the challenges posed by trade liberalization.

Much could be done, of course, on a voluntary basis, if developed countries and developing countries in a position to do so provide full duty-free quota-free (DF-QF) treatment in favor of LDCs and if developed countries start with the immediate elimination of all forms of export subsidies (as agreed to during the Hong Kong Ministerial Conference of December 2005, foreseen by the end of 2013). This would be an important step towards mitigating the effects of the global financial crisis on the poorest and most vulnerable.

But voluntary measures are not a substitute for binding commitments because they can be withdrawn at any time, and the threat of such withdrawal can be used as an important political and negotiating weapon.

Supporting South-South trade can also make a big difference for developing countries during the global economic recession, since these trade flows have been increasing well above world trade average growth. They contribute to export diversification and improvements in the value-added chain, and they are becoming a significant source of dynamism for the regional and global economy. More attention should be paid to enhancing the Global System of Trade Preferences among developing countries (GSTP), along with additional and nonconditional facilities for South-South trade financing.

In devising a Doha Round "Aid for Trade" (AFT) package, a set of baseline rules are called for: they should not be construed as a substitute for the development gains to be derived from negotiations on market access and the approval of balanced trade rules; they should be funded with additional resources either on concessional terms or in grant form; they should be provided without conditionalities other than those implicit in adhering to the Doha agreement and taking into account the specificities of each country; and they should be commitments enforceable like other commitments in the Trade Agreements. Accordingly, the governance structure of the World Bank and IMF funds created to administer Aid for Trade should be markedly different, with full voice given to the recipients.

Mechanisms for monitoring respect for and implementation of Special and Differential Treatment provisions as well as for allowing members to request AFT in accordance with their own priorities and needs should be created as an integral part of the Doha Round "single undertaking."

Further tightening of intellectual property protection beyond the standards set in the Trade-Related Aspects of Intellectual Property Rights (TRIPS) Agreement, or imposing trade-distorting or public health–threatening levels of intellectual property (IP) enforcement that negatively affect access to medicines by poor developing countries, would certainly not be a welcome result in any negotiation premised on a development perspective. What is positive in this sense about the Doha Round is that changes to IP obligations are not on the negotiating table except for two very specific and narrowly defined areas, of which one, an amendment to the TRIPS Agreement to mitigate bio piracy and protect genetic resources traditional knowledge, has actually become a point of proactive negotiation by the virtual majority of developing countries members of the WTO. A mandatory requirement for disclosure of the country providing/source of genetic resources and mechanisms such as Access and Benefit Sharing and Prior Informed Consent should be implemented in the TRIPS Agreement.

An agreement on modalities for concluding the Doha Round has to be sufficiently broad to create a critical mass of bargaining elements that would allow developed members to overcome long entrenched domestic lobbies that otherwise will resist the call for the elimination and reduction of trade-distorting subsidies.

A successful conclusion of the Doha Round would set the basis for further work adapting the WTO to the ever-changing needs of the world economy. But as we have noted, a successful conclusion must go some way to meeting the original commitments that it be a development round.[4] A discussion on possible reforms of the WTO itself should directly be addressed after the conclusion of the Round.

5

INTERNATIONAL
FINANCIAL INNOVATIONS

Previous chapters have analyzed the macroeconomic policy and regulatory reforms needed to guarantee a sustainable and development-friendly recovery of the world economy. Chapter 4 looked at reforms of current financial institutions and broader institutional innovations. This chapter confronts another set of innovations to improve the global reserve system, manage sovereign debt defaults, better distribute the risks between lenders and borrowers in world markets, and create novel financing mechanisms for development cooperation and the provision of global public goods.

THE GLOBAL RESERVE SYSTEM

Since the breakdown of the Bretton Woods system with the suspension of the gold convertibility of the dollar in 1971, a system of flexible exchange rates among major currencies has predominated. Although alternative national and regional currencies (such as the euro) compete with each other as international reserve assets and means of international settlement, the dollar has maintained its predominant role in both regards. This system has proven to be unstable, incompatible with global full employment, and inequitable.

One of the main problems of the Bretton Woods system was identified by Robert Triffin in the 1950s: the use of a *national* currency (the US dollar) as the *international* reserve currency. This generated a difficult dilemma since the dollar deficits necessary to increase global liquidity eroded confidence in the dollar as a reserve currency and created doubt about the ability of the U.S. to maintain dollar-gold parity. Abandonment of dollar convertibility and the acceptance of flexible exchange rates eliminated some of these problems but at the same time created new ones. Instead of uncertainty over the ability to maintain dollar-gold parity, the "Triffin dilemma" has been reflected in large swings in U.S. current account imbalances and associated volatility of the dollar exchange rate and, in the long-run, with the risk of loss in the value of foreign exchange reserves held in dollars as U.S. external deficits increased.

Instability and the inability to guarantee full employment have arguably worsened after the introduction of flexible exchange rates. Floating exchange rates have not been able to eliminate the deflationary bias associated with the greater pressure on deficit countries than surplus countries to adjust to payments imbalances. The exception is, of course, the country issuing the dominant international reserve currency, which can actually generate during some periods the opposite phenomenon—an inflationary bias associated with excess dollar liquidity. As pointed out in the previous paragraph, though, this bias comes at the cost of dollar exchange rate volatility and eventual erosion in the value of dollar assets. The relaxation of controls on capital flows that accompanied more flexible exchange regimes has introduced new forms of instability associated with the volatility of capital flows and particularly, but not only, short-term flows.

As a result of a sequence of severe crises experienced since the breakdown of the Bretton Woods system, a number of developing countries, particularly in Asia and Latin America, have sought new instruments to protect themselves against global financial and economic instability. Coupled with the increasing unwillingness of developing countries to submit to the conditionalities associated with IMF lending, this has led to a massive accumulation of reserves over the past two decades. As these reserves are mostly held in hard currencies, they also represent a transfer of resources to the United States and other industrialized countries.

Many believe that the problems of the current reserve system could be eliminated by creating a supranational international reserve currency. Indeed, the idea of an international reserve currency issued by a supranational bank is not new. It was broached more than 75 years ago by John Maynard Keynes in his 1930 *Treatise on Money* and refined in his Bretton Woods proposal for an International Clearing Union.

There currently exist a number of alternative proposals for a new global reserve currency, for how the system might be administered, how the emissions of the new currency might be allocated, and how the transition to the new system might be best managed. Considerable discussion will be required for the international community to decide the precise arrangements. However, this is an idea whose time has come. This is a feasible proposal and it is imperative that the international community begins working on the creation of such a new global reserve system. A failure to do so will jeopardize prospects for a stable international monetary and financial system, which is necessary to support a return to robust and stable growth.

Instability

The operation of the current international system has been marred by a number of sources of instability. As noted, it has been unable to constrain the size of payments imbalances that have led to large holdings of the international reserve currency. This in turn has led to deterioration in confidence in the dollar's role as a global store of value. After the abandonment of fixed exchange rates in the early 1970s, the main manifestation of expanding domestic demand and "excess" dollar liquidity was a decline in confidence in the dollar. When this led to measures by the U.S. to reduce dollar liquidity, in part to restore the credibility of the dollar's reserve currency status, it generated dollar appreciation and contractionary pressures on the world economy. Two additional cycles of excess dollar liquidity, followed by U.S. adjustment, were also experienced in the following decades. U.S. monetary policies have been implemented with little consideration of their impact on global aggregate demand or demands for global liquidity and are thus a potential cause of instability in exchange rates and global activity.

Since the 1960s, the system has indeed been plagued with cycles of diminished confidence in the U.S. dollar. These cycles have become particularly intense since the 1980s, leading to unprecedented volatility both in the U.S. current account deficit and the effective exchange rate of the U.S. dollar. As a result, the major attribute of an international store of value and reserve asset, a stable external value, has been eroded.

There is another sense in which the current system is unstable. By definition, for the world economy, the sum of all deficit countries' balance of payments must equal the sum of all other countries' surpluses. But the way surpluses and deficits are brought into equality is not necessarily smooth and will usually involve changes in incomes of individual countries. If a large number of countries choose policies aimed at increasing their trade surpluses, or if international institutions encourage deficit countries to improve their balance of payments, the deficits of the remaining country or countries will become increasingly large. With the dollar as the major international reserve currency, if the rest of the world seeks to run external surpluses, this will result in a decline in global income, unless the U.S. is willing to be the "deficit country of last resort." In turn, if U.S. macroeconomic policies are overtly expansionary and the rest of the world is unwilling to accumulate dollar assets, the adjustment will also take place through downward adjustment in global income. In either case the result is likely to be growing global imbalances, exchange rate instability, and erosion of confidence in the dollar as a reserve currency.

The introduction of flexible exchange rates in the presence of growing private international capital flows failed to meet the expectation that adjustment of the balance of payments would become smoother while leaving each country the necessary autonomy to guarantee their domestic macroeconomic policy objectives. The basic reason is that countries can avoid adjustment as long as they can attract sufficient external flows. When these prove to be insufficient to fund the imbalance or are reversed because of lack of confidence in the deficit countries, the adjustment takes the form of a financial crisis. The asymmetry remains, but the negative impact on the deficit countries is much greater, as the increasing frequency and severity of financial crises since the mid-1970s have made clear.

Self-Insurance and Deflationary Bias

Global imbalances, associated in part with the way different countries reacted to the financial instability of the late 1990s and early 2000s, played an important role in the macroeconomic conditions leading to the current world financial crisis. The asymmetric adjustments to these global imbalances played a part in generating the insufficiency of global aggregate demand that has helped convert a U.S. financial disruption into a global economic recession. Unless both global imbalances and the insufficiency of aggregate demand are remedied, it will be difficult to restore robust, stable economic growth.

Problems in the design and functioning of the international financial system led to large accumulations of reserves by developing countries in recent years, especially after the Asian and Russian crises of 1997–1998. These crises, like those that preceded them in the late 1970s and early 1980s, showed that developing and emerging countries are subject to strong pro-cyclical capital flows. If authorities react by allowing capital surges during booms to generate rapid exchange rate appreciation and the build-up of current account deficits, the outcome is almost certainly a balance of payments crisis accompanied or soon followed by a domestic financial crisis. This problem is particularly acute when the boom is in the form of largely speculative short-term capital flows, a point that came to be increasingly recognized after the Asian crisis. The decision to build stronger current account positions and to accumulate large foreign exchange reserves in the face of booming capital inflows in 2004–2007 were therefore often a common response of these countries to reduce the likelihood that they would face crises and to create policy space to respond if they occurred.

Similarly, commodity-exporting countries have experienced repeated crises, when improvements in the terms of trade lead to unsustainable demand expansion and exchange rate appreciation that generates "Dutch disease" effects. As a result, since the Asian crisis, commodity exporting developing countries, as well as export-oriented economies more generally, have tried to avoid exchange rate appreciation by saving part of the exceptional export proceeds considered to be temporary. High commodity prices in the boom years preceding the current crisis exacerbated the problems that this posed for global balances.

These policies could be considered as "self-insurance" or "self-protection" against reversals of capital flows, adverse movements in the terms of trade, excessive exchange rate volatility, and the associated risks of balance of payments and domestic financial crises. The fact that the only available "collective insurance" is IMF financial assistance, which is highly conditional, often imposing pro-cyclical policies during crises, reinforced the view that self-protection in the form of reserve accumulation was a better strategy.[5]

As a result of these factors, reserve accumulations rose to 11.7% of world GDP in 2007, compared to 5.6% a decade earlier when the Asian crisis struck. Reserve accumulations in the period 2003–2007, in the run up to the current crisis, amounted to an annual average of $777 billion a year, or 1.6% of global GDP. The major concern is that if the current crisis is as long and as deep as feared, and if the assistance provided to developing countries is inadequate, there will be attempts to preserve strong external balances through protectionist measures, beggar-thy-neighbor exchange rate policies, and stronger "self-insurance" through reserve accumulation. All these measures reduce global aggregate demand and impede a rapid response to the crisis.

When reserve accumulation is the result of current account surpluses and not simply the result of tempering the impact of autonomous private foreign capital inflows on the exchange rate, there is a reduction in global aggregate demand.[6] In the past, the negative impact of these reserve accumulations on global aggregate demand was offset by other countries' large current account deficits, particularly due to loose monetary and fiscal policies in the United States. But the outcome, as we have seen, has been global instability. Today, most countries eschew these policies.

The question posed by the autonomous reduction of the United States' deficit now under way is: what will sustain global aggregate demand? It is unlikely to be another American bubble leading to another period of large and unsustainable American deficits and the continuation of global imbalances. Such a course risks a repeat of the current crisis. Thus, something has to be done about the underlying sources of the insufficiency of global aggregate demand.

A global reserve currency whose creation is not linked to the external position of any particular national economy could provide a better system to manage the instability analyzed above. It should be designed to regulate the creation of global liquidity and maintain global macroeconomic stability. It would also make the problems noted above related to the creation of excess liquidity by the reserve currency country less likely to occur. Reforms in the global financial system should also include innovations to improve risk-sharing mechanisms that would reduce the demand for reserve accumulations, and thus reduce the magnitude of the requisite liquidity creation (see below).

The system should similarly be designed to put pressure on countries to reduce their surpluses and to thus reduce their contribution to the insufficiency of global aggregate demand. This would also contribute to the reduction of global imbalances.

Inequities

The current system is also inequitable because it results in developing countries transferring resources, typically at low interest rates, to the developed countries that issue the reserve currencies. In particular, the buildup of dollar reserves represents lending to the United States at very low interest rates (today close to zero). This transfer has increased over time due to the realization by developing countries that large foreign exchange reserves are their only defense in a world of acute financial and terms of trade instability.

Developing countries are, in effect, lending to developed countries large amounts at low interest rates—$3.7 trillion in 2007. The difference between the lending rate and the interest rate which these countries pay to developed countries when they borrow from them is a transfer of resources to the reserve currency countries that exceeds in value the foreign assistance that developing countries receive from the developed countries. The fact that developing countries choose to hold such reserves is testimony to their perception of the costs of instability—of the adjustment costs that they would have to bear if they did not have these reserves.

Costs to the Reserve Currency Country

The United States also incurs costs associated with its role in supplying global reserves. The demand for global reserves has led to increasing current account deficits in the United States that have had adverse effects on U.S. domestic demand; when dollars are held to meet increased demands for liquidity in surplus countries, they fail to produce any countervailing adjustment in foreign demand. This necessitates the U.S. maintaining persistent fiscal deficits, if it wishes to keep the economy at or near full employment—with the exception of periods of "irrational exuberance," such as the tech bubble of the late 1990s. In addition, the periodic need to correct these deficits requires contractionary monetary or fiscal policies that have adverse domestic effects on the U.S. economy.

Countries holding substantial dollar reserves have called for assurances that the U.S. authorities do not allow any depreciation in the international value of the dollar and thus a decline in the value of their reserve holdings. China, the major holder of dollar reserves, has already noted the risks to its dollar reserves should the U.S. adopt policies leading to depreciation of the dollar. The only way to respond to this call would involve a loss of policy autonomy for the U.S., as it would have to take into consideration the effects of its monetary policy on the rest of the world and their perceptions of these impacts. Maintaining U.S. monetary policy autonomy, as would be required to respond effectively to the current crisis, is a major reason for the U.S. to move to a global reserve system, in addition to the benefits it would receive from a more stable global financial and economic system and from the reduction in its domestic aggregate demand (as a result of the trade deficit), with all of the adverse consequences that follow. These disadvantages more than offset the advantages that may accrue to the U.S. from its ability to borrow at low interest rates. Besides, if confidence in the dollar as a reserve system erodes (as appears to be the case), the ability of the U.S. to continue borrowing at low interest rates may be limited.

Problems with a Multiple Currency Reserve System

It should be emphasized that a system based on multiple, competing reserve currencies would not resolve the difficulties associated with the current system, since it would not solve the problems associated with national currencies—and, particularly, currencies from major industrial countries—being used as reserve assets.

The basic advantage of a multi-polar reserve world is, of course, that it provides room for diversification. However, it would come at the cost of adding an additional element of instability: the exchange rate volatility among currencies used as reserve assets. If central banks and private agents were to respond to exchange rate fluctuations by changing the composition of their international assets, this would feed into exchange rate instability. Under these conditions, the response to the introduction of a multiple currency reserve system might be calls for a return to a fixed exchange rate arrangement. But fixing the exchange rates among major currencies in a world of free capital mobility would be a daunting task that would require policy coordination and loss of monetary policy sovereignty that seems unlikely under current political conditions.

Furthermore, it would be particularly problematic for countries that are restrained in their monetary and fiscal policies (as Europe may be with its Growth and Stability Pact and with a central bank committed to focusing on inflation) to become reserve currencies, for they would face difficulties in offsetting the adverse effects on national aggregate demand arising from the associated trade deficits.

Call for a Global Reserve Currency

These long-standing deficiencies in existing arrangements have become manifest in the period leading up to the current global financial crisis and can make the crisis deeper. If countries choose increased savings and higher international reserves as a response to the uncertainty of global market conditions, this would further deepen the aggregate demand problem the world economy is now facing.

The increases in the U.S. national debt and the size of the balance sheet of the U.S. Federal Reserve have led to concerns in those countries holding large dollar reserves about the stability of the dollar as a store of value. In addition, the low (near zero) return on dollar holdings means that they are receiving virtually no return in exchange for the foreign exchange rate risk which they bear. However, any attempt to reduce dollar holdings will produce the Triffin dilemma noted earlier, provoking the collapse in the value of their dollar holdings that they fear.

These are among the reasons to adopt a truly global reserve currency. Such a global reserve system can also reduce global risks, since confidence in and stability of the reserve currency would not depend on the vagaries of the economy and politics of a single country.

The current crisis provides, in turn, an ideal opportunity to overcome the political resistance to a new global monetary system. It has brought home problems posed by global imbalances, international instability, and the current insufficiency of global aggregate demand. A global reserve system is a critical step in addressing these problems and in ensuring that, as the global economy recovers, it moves onto a path of strong growth without setting the stage for another crisis in the future. It is also a propitious moment because the United States may find its reserve currency status increasingly costly and untenable. The dollar can be a reserve currency only if others are willing to hold it as such, and as the return falls and the risk increases, greater reservations about the dollar as a reserve currency are being expressed. The dollar reserve system is likely to fray, if it is not already doing so. Moreover, the U.S. has embarked on a response to the crisis that will involve large domestic imbalances and also potentially large external imbalances, with unpredictable implications for the international reserve system. Thus, both the United States and foreign exchange reserve holding countries may actually find it acceptable to introduce a new system. The former would be able to make policy decisions with less concern about their global impact; the latter would be less concerned about the impact of U.S. policies on their reserve holdings.

Institutional Frameworks for a New Global Reserve System

In setting up such a system, a number of details need to be worked out, including who would issue the reserve currency, in what amounts, to whom, and under what conditions.

The issues are largely separable. Responsibility for managing the global reserve system could be given to the IMF, which currently issues the only global currency, Special Drawing Rights (SDRs), on which the system could be built. But it could also be given to a new institution, such as a "Global Reserve Bank." If we turn to existing institutions, this could be contingent on needed reforms of these institutions.

One possible approach would require countries to agree to exchange their own currencies for the new currency—say International Currency Certificates (ICCs), which could be SDRs—and vice versa, in much the same way as IMF quotas are made up today (except that developing countries would only make their quota contributions in their own national currencies and would thus be exempted from making part of such contributions in SDRs or convertible currencies as is the rule today). This proposal would be equivalent to a system of worldwide "swaps" among central banks. The global currency would thus be fully backed by a basket of the currencies of all members.

In an alternative approach, the international agency in charge of creating global reserves would simply issue the global currency, allocating ICCs to member countries, much as IMF Special Drawing Rights are issued today. There would be no "backing" for the global currency, except the commitment of central banks to accept it in exchange for their own currencies. This is what would give the ICCs (or SDRs) the character of an international reserve currency, the same way that acceptance by citizens of payments in a national currency gives it the character of domestic money. However, if the issues of global currency received by countries are considered deposits in the IMF or the Global Reserve Bank, and the institution in charge of managing the system is allowed to buy the government bonds of member countries or to lend to them, then these investments would be the "backing" of the global currency, just as domestic monies are "backed" today by the assets of national central banks (the government bonds in their hands and their lending to private sector financial institutions).[7]

Under any of these schemes, countries could agree to hold a certain fraction of their reserves in the global currency. The global reserve currency could also pay interest, at a rate attractive enough to induce its use as an investment for central banks' reserves. Exchange rates would be managed according to the rules that each country chooses, subject to the condition that exchange rate management does not affect other countries—a rule that is already included in the IMF Articles of Agreement and must be subject to appropriate surveillance. As with SDRs, the exchange rate of the global currency would be the weighted average of a basket of convertible currencies, the composition of which would have to be agreed.

In the alternative, in which the global currency is considered to be a deposit in the IMF or Global Reserve Bank, earnings by these institutions' investments (lending to countries undergoing balance of payments' crises, or otherwise via Treasury securities of member countries) would finance the interest paid to those countries that hold deposits of the global currency (possibly in excess of the original issues they received). Obviously the major advantage to holding the global currency is that the diversification away from individual currencies would generate more stability in the value of reserve holdings.

The global currency could be allocated to countries on the basis of some formula ("quota") based on their weight in the world economy (GDP) or their needs (some estimation of the demand for reserves). Since developing countries hold reserves which are, in proportion to their GDP, several times those of industrial countries (26.4% of GDP in 2007 vs. 4.8% for high-income OECD countries), to manage the trade and capital account volatility they face, a formula that would allocate the currency according to some definition of demand for reserves would result in larger proportional allocations to these countries. One possibility is, of course, to give developing countries all allocations. Note that the current SDR allocation is based on a particular "quota" system, that of the IMF, which continues to be subject to heated debate because richer countries, on average, get a larger share of new allocations—i.e., the opposite to what a criterion based on need would suggest.

The allocation can and should have built into it incentives and/or penalties to discourage maintaining large surpluses. Countries that maintain excessive surpluses could lose all or part of their quota allocations if they are not utilized in a timely manner to increase global demand.

The size of the annual emissions should be targeted to offset the increase in (non-borrowed) reserves, i.e., reductions in global purchasing power resulting from reserve accumulations. Simpler versions of this proposal would have annual emissions fixed at a given rate of say $150 to $300 billion a year (the first figure corresponds to the world demand for reserves in 1998–2002, but the demand for reserves was much larger in 2003–2007, suggesting that even $300 billion a year might be insufficient).

More sophisticated and elaborate versions of this proposal would have emissions adjusted in a countercyclical way, with larger emissions when global growth is below potential. It might be easier to get global consensus on either of these simpler variants, but more detailed versions would be able to support a variety of global needs (e.g., to generate badly needed revenues for development or global public goods).

One institutional way of establishing a new global reserve system is simply a broadening of existing SDR arrangements, making their issuance automatic and regular. Doing so could be viewed simply as completing the process begun in the 1960s, when SDRs were created. The simplest version, as noted, is an annual issuance equivalent to the estimated additional demand for foreign exchange reserves due to the growth of the world economy. But they could be issued in a counter-cyclical fashion, thereby concentrating issuances during crisis periods. One advantage of using SDRs in such a counter-cyclical fashion is that it would provide a mechanism for the IMF to play a more active role during crises.

Still another mechanism to manage SDRs in a counter-cyclical way was suggested by IMF economist Jacques Polak three decades ago: providing all financing during crises with SDR loans. This would generate emissions that would be automatically extinguished once loans are paid back and create the global equivalent to what the central banks of industrial countries have been doing on a massive scale during recent months.

Indeed, a large counter-cyclical issue of SDRs is the best mechanism to finance world liquidity and official support to developing countries during the current crisis. This was recognized by the G-20 in its decision to issue the equivalent of $250 billion in SDRs. However, this decision also illustrates the problems associated with tying

SDR issuance to IMF quotas, as somewhat less than $100 billion of the proposed emissions would benefit developing countries, with even a much smaller amount (about $20 billion) going to low-income countries. This implies that this issue is closely tied to the ongoing debate about reform of IMF quotas. None of the proposed reforms to quotas deal adequately with the issue of equity or indicate that different rules may have to be applied to quotas and SDR issues, as noted above.

Although developing countries would receive only part of the allocations, the capacity of the IMF to lend would be considerably enhanced if the current system was reformed in such a way that unutilized SDRs, particularly from industrial countries, could be used by the IMF to lend to member countries in need—such as the proposal of treating unused SDRs as deposits in the IMF. However, unless there are strong reforms in the IMF's practices, the ability of the emissions to address the liquidity and macroeconomic management problems noted earlier might be impaired, as developing countries might be reluctant to turn to the IMF for funds. Reforms in that direction were adopted in March 2009 with the creation of the Flexible Credit Line with only ex-ante conditionality, the doubling of all credit lines, and the elimination of structural benchmarks in conditional IMF lending. But additional reforms to make access less onerous will be needed.

A simple way to further the use of SDR allocations to advance developmental objectives (which might require changing the Articles of Agreement) would be for the International Monetary and Finance Committee and the IMF Board to allow the IMF to invest some of the funds made available through issuance of SDRs in bonds issued by multilateral development banks. This would be similar to the proposal for a "development link" made by the UNCTAD panel of experts in the 1960s (see below).

Thus, a well-designed global currency system would go a long way to correct the "Triffin dilemma" and the tendency of the current system to generate large global imbalances and the deflationary biases characteristic of balance of payments adjustments during crises. Depending on the way emissions are allocated, the system could also correct the inequities associated with the large demand for reserves by developing countries, provide collective insurance against future shocks, help finance global public goods, including the costs of climate change mitigation and adaptation, and promote development and poverty alleviation, including in the poorest countries. If emissions were issued in a counter-cyclical way, they could perform an even more important role in stabilization.

Historical Antecedents

When Keynes revised his idea of a global currency in his proposal for an International Clearing Union, as part of the preparations for what became known as the Bretton Woods Conference, his major concern was the elimination of asymmetric adjustment between deficit and surplus countries leading to the tendency towards deficiency of global aggregate demand and a constraint on the policy space needed for policies in support of full employment. He also had in mind the significant payments imbalances that, he feared, would characterize the post-war order and therefore the need to provide a better source of liquidity, both globally and for countries that would leave the war with structural payments deficits. Of course, the first of these problems, the asymmetric adjustment, was not corrected by the Bretton Woods system, and the second, the adequate provision of global liquidity, was only partly corrected.

In turn, when SDRs were created in the 1960s, the major concern was how to provide a more reliable source of global liquidity to replace gold and reserve currency holdings (mainly dollars, but also British pound sterling at the time). It was believed that the existing sources of international liquidity were not reliable, as they depended in the first case on gold production and in the second on deficits of the reserve currency countries, particularly the United States. As the initial problems of global liquidity—the "dollar shortage"—were overcome, attention shifted to risks of excessive dollar liquidity, particularly that U.S. gold reserves would not be sufficient to support dollar-gold convertibility. This finally generated the demise of the Bretton Woods "dollar-gold exchange standard" in 1971 and the adoption of flexible exchange rates among major currencies in 1973.

At the time SDRs were created, it was hoped they would become a major component of global reserves, thus creating a system in which the growth of global liquidity would depend on deliberate international decisions. This expectation was not fulfilled, and a total of only 21.4 billion SDRs (about $33 billion) were issued in two different periods (1970–72 and 1979–81), which represent only a minimal fraction of current world reserves. The recent approval by the IMF of a new emission of SDRs, for the equivalent of $250 billion, thus constitutes a major step to enhance this instrument of international cooperation.

The nature of the problems of global liquidity provision was obviously transformed with the development of private financial markets in Eurodollars and other European currencies and the introduction of a flexible exchange rate system. These problems associated with the provision of global liquidity are less important today, except during extraordinary conjunctures such as those generated by the severe shortage of liquidity, including the global liquidity crisis in August 1998 and the world financial crisis since September 2008. But a major problem remains: dependence of global liquidity on the vagaries of U.S. macroeconomic policies and balance of payments' imbalances, which can generate either excessive or limited world liquidity. The recurrent problem of developing country access to international liquidity is still a feature of the system as a result of pro-cyclical capital flows.

In Keynes's initial proposal for a post-war arrangement, there was no need to address the problem of equity in issuance since the creation of clearing credits was entirely endogenous. This question was also evaded in the initial issuances of SDRs, although some ideas were proposed at the time on how to tie the issuance of a global currency to development financing, particularly in the proposal made by an UNCTAD expert panel to link the question of liquidity provision for developed economies to the needs of developing economies for development financing. But, as already seen, equity issues cannot be ignored today because of the magnitude of the inequities associated with the current system in subjecting developing countries to recurrent problems of illiquidity or inducing them to accumulate large amounts of foreign exchange reserves.

Transition to New System

The reform of the global reserve system could take place through a global agreement or through more evolutionary approaches, including those that could build on a series of regional initiatives.

If a large enough group of countries agreed to pool reserves in a system they agreed to create and to hold a common reserve currency which they would stand ready to exchange for their own currencies, a regional reserve system—or even a system of near-global coverage—could be established without the agreement of all countries. So long as the new currency is convertible into any hard currency that is itself convertible into other currencies, it could serve effectively as a reserve currency. The countries participating might also agree to reduce, over time, their holdings of other reserve currencies.

Membership in this new "Reserve Currency Association" could be open to all who subscribe to its Articles of Agreement. The advantages of participation are sufficiently great that it is likely to grow over time, embracing more countries that hold a greater fraction of their reserves in the new global reserve currency. Eventually, even the United States would probably find it desirable to join. Thus, gradually, through a stable, evolutionary process, we can achieve the creation of a new Global Reserve System, an alternative to the current system. Of course, there is also a risk of adverse selection—as long as participation is voluntary, soft currency countries would be more willing to participate, and convertible global currencies outside the scheme could remain the preferred currencies.

Existing regional agreements might provide an alternative way of evolving towards a Global Reserve System. Regional mechanisms have advantages of their own, and can be based either on swap arrangements among central banks or on foreign exchange reserve pools. Given the reluctance of governments to give up control over their reserves, swap arrangements may be more acceptable. Reserve pools offer, however, other advantages, such as the possibility of allowing the reserve fund to borrow during periods of stress, and, as noted, to issue a currency or reserve asset that could be used at a regional or global level. In the 1980s, for example, the Latin American Reserve Fund (FLAR) was allowed to issue Andean pesos.[8] This asset, which has never been used, was expected to be used in intra-regional trade, with periodic clearing of those held by central banks. The Chiang Mai Initiative, created in 2000 by members of ASEAN, China, Japan and the Republic of Korea, is another important example of regional cooperation.[9] Were this initiative to evolve into a reserve fund, it could back the issuance of a regional asset that could actually be attractive to central banks in other parts of the world to hold as part of their reserve assets. However, if the Chiang Mai Initiative is to play a more effective role in stabilization, it would be necessary to eliminate the requirement that countries would need to have an IMF program to qualify for access to its swap facilities.

A common criticism of regional arrangements is that they are not effective in providing diversification for protection against systemic crisis, as regional members are more likely to be adversely affected at the same time, implying that they are a complement to, rather than a substitute for, a global solution. Although the ability of regional arrangements to address external shocks depends on negative events not being correlated across participating countries, they could still be useful if shocks affect member countries with different intensities or with varying lags, since this would allow some countries to lend their reserves to those experiencing more severe or earlier shocks. Furthermore, lending at the onset of a liquidity squeeze could prevent a crisis in a given country from affecting other countries, thereby reducing the correlation produced by contagion. More generally, a country would benefit from the regional arrangement if the variability of the regional reserve pool is lower than that of its individual reserves and if potential access to the pool reduces the possibility of attacks on individual members. These regional arrangements thus act as a mechanism of collective insurance that is substantially more powerful than self-insurance. Statistical analysis by the UN Economic Commission for Latin American and the Caribbean supports the benefits that accrue from this approach, by indicating that correlations of relevant macroeconomic variables among countries in the region may be lower than usually assumed.

Regional initiatives could become part and parcel of the global reserve system. Some have suggested that the reformed IMF should be a network of such regional reserve funds. Such a decentralized system would have many advantages, including the possibility of better solving problems associated with crises in the smaller countries at the regional level. The system would also be attractive for medium and small-sized countries that could have stronger voices at the regional level. One way to link regional and global arrangements would be to make contributions to regional arrangements one factor to take into account in determining SDR allocations.

SOVEREIGN DEBT DEFAULT AND RESTRUCTURING

Inadequacies of the Existing System (or "Non-system")

Sovereign debt crises have been a major source of the difficulties faced by developing countries in achieving sustained growth and development at different times since the 1980s. The social costs of these crises have been extremely large and have included long periods of lost income and jobs, increased poverty, and, in some cases, worsening income inequality. Given the instability of external capital flows, severe financial crises have even hit countries judged by international opinion to have been soundly managed. In several cases, crises originated from governments taking over the responsibility for servicing private-sector debts of the banking system or key firms judged "too big to fail"—in a way not too different from how the U.S. and other industrial country governments have done during the current global crisis. Such "nationalization" of private sector external debt was a feature of the Latin American debt crisis of the 1980s and has been quite common in developing-country debt crises since then.

Not only are current "workout" processes protracted and costly, but often, the debt write-downs have also been insufficient to ensure debt sustainability. The existence of debt overhangs depresses growth, contributes to poverty, and crowds out essential public services. Often, when write-downs have been insufficient, they are soon followed by another crisis. And because of the adverse terms and high costs imposed by debt workouts, developing countries are reluctant to default in a timely way, resulting in delays in dealing with the underlying problems.

Moreover, worries about a protracted crisis in one country having spillover effects for others have motivated massive bailouts, contributing in turn to problems of moral hazard and enhancing the likelihood of future crises.

Whatever the explanation of these crises (whether they are due to risky policies on the part of governments or the intensified economic fluctuations of liberalized financial environments), the existing system of protracted, creditor-biased resolution of sovereign debt crises is not in the global public interest and far from the interests of the poor in the affected countries.

The existing "system" (or really "non-system") arose as piecemeal and mostly ad hoc intergovernmental responses to sovereign debt crises as they occurred over the past half-century or so. The fact that the solutions the current system provides take time to be adopted and provide inadequate relief implies that the system for addressing sovereign debtors is clearly inferior to that provided in many countries for corporations and sub-sovereign public entities by national bankruptcy regimes. The latter aims to find not only a quick and equitable solution that recognizes the claims of formal creditors as well as the rights of ordinary citizens, e.g., to education, health, or old age benefits, but also a solution that achieves nationally desired economic and social outcomes, particularly a "fresh start" (or "clean slate") when a bankrupt entity is reorganized. In contrast, the system for resolving sovereign debt crises is plagued by horizontal inequities. Official lenders have always complained that private creditors do not follow restructurings agreed in the Paris Club (and have been "free riders"). The magnitude of debt rescheduling and relief accorded in individual cases has clearly depended on the weight and negotiating capacity of the debtor country.

The system for sovereign debtors has operated under the informal and imperfect coordination of the debtor and its creditors by the IMF, under the guidance of the G-7 major industrialized countries, which set the overall policy directions for the IMF and the other involved institutions, such as the Paris Club, where debts owed to governments are restructured. The system assumes a developing country government in debt distress will adopt an IMF-approved macroeconomic adjustment program, that the program will be effective, and that all the relevant classes of creditors (banks, bondholders and suppliers, government creditors, and multilateral institutions) will cooperate in providing the overall amount of relief and financial support deemed necessary on the basis of IMF documents. Often there is very little real debt relief, only a rescheduling of obligations, and the magnitude of relief is based on excessively optimistic growth projections—setting the stage for problems down the line.

Since these basic conditions for the successful implementation of debt relief were seldom met, confidence in the system has quickly eroded and was severely affected by how the East Asian, Russian, Ecuadorian, and Argentine crises were handled. Even the Heavily Indebted Poor Countries (HIPC) Initiative as initially instituted was recognized to be insufficient to give the poorest countries a fresh start. After almost a decade of negotiations, it was supplemented in 2005 with the Multilateral Debt Relief Initiative. Nevertheless, the HIPC Initiative represented the first comprehensive approach to a solution of the debt problems of poor developing countries. The initiative came along with a framework that placed poverty reduction strategies at the center of development cooperation, based in part on a dialogue including the participation of civil society. Nevertheless, pro-cyclical conditionalities were often applied, which had damaging effects on socioeconomic conditions.

Apart from that, some individual non-HIPC renegotiations that took place after the East Asian crisis have been judged as unsatisfactory. Most single country "workouts" from debt crises in this period were under cooperative voluntary arrangements with the bondholders that did not reduce the level of debt. The transparency of some of these renegotiation processes—including the pressures exerted on debtor countries by other nations and IFIs—has also been questioned.

Moreover, while creditors have a seat at the table, other claimants—such as government retirees who have been promised a particular level of pensions—do not. Chapter 9 of the U.S. bankruptcy code, which applies to municipalities and other sub-sovereign public entities, gives priority to these "public" claimants on government revenues. In contrast, international procedures seem to pay insufficient attention to such interests.

Finally, some critics of current practices suggest that they are unnecessarily "painful" because they are designed to provide strong incentives for countries not to default on their obligations. Small and weak countries are more likely to be forced to pay the price for ensuring that the overall system exercises discipline on borrowers.

Argentina's rapid growth after its 2001 default, in spite of the long delay to the final resolution, shows that eliminating debt overhang can provide conditions for rapid economic growth even in seemingly adverse conditions. Despite rapid growth, however, this country faced significant problems regaining access to private financial markets.

AN INTERNATIONAL DEBT RESTRUCTURING COURT

Some have argued that new debt restructuring procedures are not needed; all that is required are small reforms in debt contracts, such as collective action clauses. But no country relies solely on collective action clauses for debt resolution, and there is no reason to believe that doing so for international debt would be sufficient. For instance, collective action clauses do not provide effective means for resolving conflicts among different classes of claimants.

It is easy to agree that the amount of debt relief accorded to different countries should depend on their circumstances. However, it is artificial to have one set of rules for determining relief for selected developing countries, as was the case for the HIPCs and then for the Multilateral Debt Relief Initiative, and another for the rest of the world. Rather, a single statutory framework for debt relief is needed to ensure that creditors and debtors restructure the debt to provide a fresh start based on a country's unique economic conditions. The debt workout regime should be efficient, equitable, transparent, and timely in handling debt problems ex post (as problems become apparent, especially after default) while promoting efficiency ex ante (when the borrowing takes place).

A well-designed process should protect the rights of minority, as well as majority, creditors—as well as "public" claimants. It should give debtors the opportunity to default through a structured process. The principles of human-centered development, of sustainability, and of equity in the treatment of debtors and their creditors and among creditors should apply equally to all sovereign debt crises resolved through the international system. As in national bankruptcy systems, principals should be encouraged to reach a workout on their own to the extent possible. But whether such an agreement can be reached, and the nature of the agreement, can be affected by the backdrop of legal structures.

Achieving these objectives requires a more structured framework for international cooperation in this area. For the same reason that governments adopt bankruptcy legislation and do not rely solely on voluntary processes for resolving corporate bankruptcies, an efficient sovereign system requires something more than a moral appeal to cooperation. This means the creation of a sovereign debt workout mechanism.

This entails the creation of an "International Debt Restructuring Court," similar to national bankruptcy courts. This court would ensure that agreed international principles regarding the priority of claims, necessary overall write-downs, and sharing of "haircuts" are followed. It could differentiate between distinct debt categories, which might include government, government-guaranteed, and government-acquired private debt, so as to make transparent the actual effective liabilities of the sovereign. It could also determine what debts could be considered "odious," and it would be able to grant potential private or public creditors authority to extend "debtor in possession" financing, as in corporate restructurings. National courts would have to recognize the legitimacy of the international court, and both creditors and debtors will therefore follow its rulings.

As an interim step in the creation of the International Debt Restructuring Court, an International Mediation Service might be created—a kind of "soft" law to facilitate the creation of norms for sovereign debt restructurings, recognizing that to a large extent compliance with international law and the repayment of sovereign debts is, in some sense, "voluntary."

Even after the creation of the court, there is a presumption that judicial proceedings would be preceded by mediation. With a view to realizing a comprehensive workout, the court would encourage creditors to coordinate their positions within and across different classes of lenders, including in the long-run the government creditors that operate today through the Paris Club as well as multilateral creditors. Were mediation to fail or become unduly lengthy, the court should have the power to arbitrate. The court might also work in cooperation with the IMF, the World Bank, or regional development banks to help provide interim finance in order to maintain economic strength while negotiations take place. But such lending should not be a mechanism simply for bailing out creditors who failed to do due diligence in providing lending.

Beyond the problems of sovereign debt restructuring, there are also serious problems in managing cross-border private debt workouts, with conflicts among different jurisdictions and with concerns about "home" country bias. The International Debt Restructuring Court could extend its reach to consider bankruptcy cases involving parties in multiple jurisdictions. (These problems have been particularly acute in the current crisis in international financial institutions operating in many jurisdictions. See the discussion in Chapter 3.)

In earlier discussions of sovereign debt restructuring mechanisms, it was presumed that the IMF, or a separate and newly established division of the IMF, would act as the bankruptcy court. However, while it may be desirable to institutionalize the sovereign debt restructuring mechanism under the umbrella of an international institution, the IMF, in its current form, is unlikely to be the appropriate institution as it is a creditor and also subject to disproportionate influence by creditor countries. It is therefore unlikely to be seen as a "neutral" mediator or arbitrator. The arbitration process of the International Centre for Settlement of Investment Disputes (ICSID) within the World Bank has similarly failed to generate confidence from the developing countries as a fair arbitrator of investor-state disputes under bilateral investment agreements.

Any procedure must be based on widely shared principles and processes with political legitimacy. Agreed-upon goals, such as that the workout must be fair, transparent, sustainable, and promote development, would boost its credibility with debtors. Indeed, all stakeholders could benefit from improved processes for restructuring debt, including creditors who would appreciate the reduction of uncertainty under clear rules of the game and the knowledge that any post-workout debt situation would have a larger chance of being sustainable. But translating these goals into agreed-upon principles and procedures may be difficult, given the conflicts in interests.[10]

Public debt audits for transparent and fair restructuring and eventual cancellations of debts should be encouraged. Norway and Ecuador provide examples.

There is nothing immutable in the current approach to resolving sovereign debt crises. It arose in the political and economic environment created after World War II, and the need to develop a better system remains on the international policy agenda. The international community needs to actively resume the effort to define the specific mechanism to institutionalize the principles advanced here.

Foreign Debt Management

The crisis also gives urgency to reform of institutional structures for debt relief as an increasing number of developing countries, especially the most vulnerable low-income countries, may face difficulties in meeting their external debt commitments. This crisis therefore gives urgency to these reforms. Unless these debts are better managed than they have been in the past, the consequences for developing countries, and especially the poor in these countries, can be serious.

Although, as argued above, there is a need for new procedures for restructuring sovereign debt, it is also important to take measures to ensure that debts that are currently being incurred are better managed. It is important to take actions to manage debt better so that countries are not forced into default.

The United Nations should therefore strengthen the UN Conference on Trade and Development's (UNCTAD) advisory role in debt management. Alternatively, the establishment of a Foreign Debt Commission that assesses external debt problems of developing countries and economies in transition could be considered. The Commission, with balanced geographic representation and technical support from the Bretton Woods, regional, and other financial institutions, would provide advice on ways to enhance external debt management and crisis prevention and resolution.[11] It would also examine existing arrangements and advise on the design of better debt sustainability frameworks for the international community. It would help debt-distressed countries return to debt sustainability, extend Paris Club–plus type approaches to new official creditors, set up an interim mediation service, and help craft more permanent debt mediation and arbitration mechanisms (i.e., the International Debt Restructuring Court) on the basis of that experience.

INNOVATIVE RISK MANAGEMENT STRUCTURES

The volatility of private capital flows to developing countries has generated increasing demand for policies and instruments that would allow these countries to better manage the risks generated by increasing international financial integration and, in particular, to better distribute the risks associated with this integration among different market agents. As demonstrated during past and current crises, the pro-cyclical and herding behavior of international capital flows tends to generate boom-bust cycles, which are particularly damaging for developing countries. Current arrangements also reduce the scope developing countries have to undertake counter-cyclical macroeconomic policies. Moreover, many developing and emerging countries borrow short-term, in hard currencies, which forces them to bear the risk of interest rate and exchange rate fluctuations. Finally, inadequate debt resolution mechanisms impose high costs on developing countries.

In light of this, there have been a variety of ideas and proposals for the introduction of innovative financial instruments. The proposed instruments include tools that enable better management of risks arising from the business cycle and fluctuations in commodity prices, particularly GDP and commodity linked bonds and financial guarantees that have a counter-cyclical element embedded in their structure. Promoting local currency bond markets has also been seen as a way to enhance financial development and reduce the currency mismatches that affect debt structures in developing countries.

GDP-linked bonds are conventional bonds that pay a low fixed coupon augmented by an additional payment, linked by a predetermined formula to the debtor country's GDP growth. This variable return structure links returns to the ability to service and thus reduces the likelihood of costly and disruptive defaults and debt crises. The reduction of a country's debt service when the economy faces financing difficulties can also facilitate more rapid recovery, as it allows higher public spending in difficult times. For investors, GDP-linked bonds reduce the probability of default and thus the costs of expensive renegotiation, and they offer a valuable diversification opportunity. Average returns might be higher than with conventional bonds, but the fact that these bonds enable countries to manage the risks which they face may more than compensate for the additional costs.[12]

Since private financial markets are unlikely to develop these instruments autonomously (because of the externalities associated with their introduction, the social returns exceed the private returns), multilateral development banks should take an active role in their development. In particular, these institutions could have an active role as "market makers." The expertise developed by the World Bank as market maker for the sale of carbon credits under the Kyoto protocol provides a precedent for these activities. The World Bank and regional development banks could, for example, make loans whose servicing would be linked to GDP. The loans could then be sold to financial markets, either individually or grouped and securitized. Alternatively, the World Bank or regional banks could buy GDP-linked bonds that developing countries would issue via private placements. The fact that major multilateral development banks became active in this type of lending could extend the benefits of adjusting debt service to growth variations to countries that do not have access to the private bond market. GDP-indexed securities are particularly appropriate for Islamic finance, as they can be made compatible with shari'a law, which prohibits charging interest.

There might also be alternative ways of ensuring flexible payment arrangements that would allow automatic adjustment for borrowers during bad times. For instance, one possibility is for coupon payments to remain fixed and for the amortization schedule to be adjusted instead. Countries would postpone part or all of their debt payments during economic downturns and would then make up by pre-paying during economic upswings. A historical precedent was set by the United Kingdom when it borrowed from the United States in the 1940s. The 1946 Anglo-American Financial Agreement included a "bisque clause" that provided a 2% interest payment waiver in any year in which the United Kingdom's foreign exchange income was not sufficient to meet its prewar level of imports, adjusted to current prices.

Commodity-linked bonds can also play a useful role in reducing country vulnerabilities, which is of special relevance to commodity exporters. Examples of commodity-indexed bonds include oil-backed bonds, such as the Brady bonds with oil warrants first issued on behalf of the government of Mexico. In such instruments, the coupon or principal payments are linked to the price of a referenced commodity. Again, it might be desirable for international institutions to help create a market for such bonds.

Developing countries may face higher debt costs as they attempt to shift commodity price risk to others, but the benefits of such risk shifting should exceed the costs if markets are working well. While they are likely to be less useful than GDP-indexed bonds for the growing number of developing countries that have a fairly diversified export structure and therefore lack a natural commodity price to link to bond payments, they have the decided advantage that the risk being "insured" through the bond is not affected by the actions of the country (i.e., moral hazard is less of a problem).

Another way of addressing the problems created by the inherent tendency of private flows to be pro-cyclical is for public institutions to provide offsetting counter-cyclical finance, possibly through the issue of guarantees that have counter-cyclical elements. For example, Multilateral Development Banks (MDBs) and Export Credit Agencies (ECAs) could introduce an explicit counter-cyclical element in guarantees they issue for lending to developing countries. When banks or other lenders lower their exposure to a country, MDBs or ECAs would increase the level of guarantees that they are willing to extend, if they consider the country's long-term fundamentals that remain to be basically sound. When matters are seen by private banks to improve and their willingness to lend increases, MDBs or ECAs could reduce their exposure. Alternatively, there could be special stand-alone guarantee mechanisms for trade and/or long-term credit—for example, within multilateral or regional development banks—which have a strong explicit counter-cyclical element. These mechanisms could be activated in periods of sharp decline in capital flows; their aim would be to try to catalyze private sector trade or provide long-term credits, especially for infrastructure.

Finally, a number of developing countries have encouraged development of domestic capital markets, particularly local currency bond markets. These markets in fact boomed after the Asian crisis, multiplying fivefold between 1997 and 2007 for the twenty large and medium-sized emerging economies for which the Bank of International Settlements provides regular information. This trend can be seen as a response of emerging economies to the volatility and procyclical bias of international capital flows and the volatility of exchange rates. It can be viewed as a means of creating a more stable source of local currency funding for both the public and private sectors, thereby mitigating the funding difficulties created by sudden stops in cross-border capital flows, reducing dependence on bank credit as a source of funding and, above all, lowering the risk of currency mismatches. For foreign investors, it could actually be attractive to form diversified portfolios of emerging market local currency debt issued by sovereign governments or developing country corporations, with a return-to-risk that competes favorably with other major capital market security indices.

Further development of these markets is desirable. First, developing countries' bond markets are still largely dominated by relatively short-term issues and therefore tend to correct currency mismatches while increasing maturity mismatches. Second, it has proved to be much easier to develop large and deep local markets for public sector debt than for corporate debt. As a result, large corporations have continued to rely on external financing. To the extent that such external financing is shorter-term than what many developing countries' governments are able to get in global debt markets, the overall debt structure of these countries tends to become shorter-term and therefore riskier. Indeed, the rollover of external corporate debt is viewed as the major problem facing many emerging economies today. Third, many of these markets are not very liquid. This problem has actually become more acute during the recent market downswing. Fourth, although local bond issues have attracted foreign investors, they were largely, or at least partly, lured by the generalized expectations of exchange rate appreciations that prevailed in many developing countries during the recent boom. As the world financial crisis hit, there were large outflows of such funds, and in this sense, reliance on these short-term portfolio flows did not correct but may have enhanced the pro-cyclicality of financing, much as short-term external bank debt did during previous crises.

Therefore, although the development of local bond markets has been a major advance in developing country financing since the Asian crisis, its promise remains partly unfulfilled in terms of risk mitigation. It is important for developing country governments, with support from international organizations, to correct some of the problems that have been evident and to continue investing in the development of deep and longer-term domestic bond markets.

INNOVATIVE SOURCES OF FINANCING

For some time, the difficulty in meeting the official UN development assistance target of 0.7% of GNI of industrial countries, as well as the need for adequate funding for the provision of global and regional public goods (peace building, fighting global health pandemics, combating climate change, and sustaining the global environment more generally) has generated proposals on how to guarantee a more reliable and stable source of financing for these objectives.

This debate has led to a heterogeneous family of initiatives. A distinguishing feature of developments in recent years is the fact that the old idea of innovative finance has lead to action, with the launching in Paris in 2006 of the "Leading Group on Solidarity Levies." The Leading Group now involves close to 60 countries and major international organizations.

Some of the initiatives proposed encompass "solidarity levies" or, more generally, taxation for global objectives. To avert their being perceived as encroachments on participating countries' fiscal sovereignty, it has been agreed that these taxes should be nationally imposed but internationally coordinated. Some countries have already decreed solidarity levies on airline tickets, but there is a larger set of proposals.

There have also been suggestions to auction global natural resources—such as ocean fishing rights and pollution emission permits—for global environmental programs.

Receipts from these innovative initiatives could be directed to support developing countries in meeting their development objectives, including their contribution to the supply of global public goods, as well as international organizations active in guaranteeing the provision of such goods. The existing taxes on airline tickets, for example, are being used to finance international programs to combat malaria, tuberculosis, and HIV/AIDS.

The proposal of taxes that could be earmarked for global objectives has a long history. While universal participation is not indispensable, it would serve the interest of development, as more resources would be raised. Some suggestions aim at both raising funds for global objectives and mitigating negative externalities at the global level. Two suggestions deserve special attention: a carbon tax and a levy on financial transactions.

Since carbon dioxide is the main contributor to global warming, a tax on its emission (or the auctioning of emission rights) can be defended on environmental efficiency grounds; it would simultaneously correct a negative externality and be a significant source of development financing. Revenues generated from the sale of emission rights in developed countries (or from the imposition of a tax in developed countries) would be transferred to developing countries, either for narrow purposes of climate change mitigation and adaptation (in fulfillment of obligations to which the developed countries have already agreed) or for broader purposes of development and poverty alleviation. The design of any tax/cap and trade system must, of course, take into account distributional impacts within countries and between countries. Some of the revenues generated would have to be devoted to ameliorating any adverse distributional impacts.

Similar mechanisms can be designed to pay for environmental services. Such schemes are already in operation locally in different areas of the world. They allow for consumers of a given public good to compensate for some of the costs borne by those producing or preserving it, and they provide incentives for the provision of the good. For instance, downstream users of water can pay those who manage the upstream forest to ensure a sustainable supply into the future. Similar instruments could pay for the provision of global environmental services, such as the conservation of rain forests. These forests play an important role both in protecting bio-diversity and in carbon sequestration. Payments to developing countries for providing these ecological services through maintaining their rain forests would provide incentives for them to continue to do so and, at the same time, provide substantial sums that could be used for development and poverty alleviation.

Taxes on pollution are an example of instruments that simultaneously raise revenue as they improve economic efficiency by correcting a negative externality. It is more efficient to tax bad things (like pollution) than good things (like work and savings). Earlier chapters have identified other negative externalities, especially those associated with excessively volatile cross-border, short-term capital flows ("hot money"). Concern about these destabilizing capital flows has led to proposals for a financial service transactions tax. Besides strong political opposition in some countries by a number of stakeholders, there are difficulties in implementation. How easy it would be to overcome these obstacles remains a subject of controversy. Some have suggested a more narrowly based tax, e.g., on trade in shares, bonds, and derivatives; because large stock exchange centers exhibit positive agglomeration externalities, a small tax imposed on transactions would not lead to a flight of trading to alternative, smaller exchanges. (A similar argument might apply to the over-the-counter trading in derivatives by large banks; again, because of the large advantages they have in lower counterparty risk, there would not be a flight to smaller institutions.)

Another set of proposals rely on the use of new financing mechanisms. One mechanism that already has a long history is swaps of debt for development objectives. It has recently been used in the Debt2Health initiative launched in Berlin in 2007, which converts portions of old debt claims on developing countries into new domestic resources for health. The International Finance Facility was proposed by the UK in 2003 to front-load commitments for future flows of ODA, by issuing bonds backed by public or private sector donor pledges. The first of these mechanisms, the International Finance Facility for Immunization, is already in place. While these mechanisms may provide more funding in the short-run, they risk shortchanging the availability of funds at later dates. Such intertemporal transfers can only be justified if: (i) the interest rate in these facilities is lower than that at which governments can borrow; and (ii) the funds are invested in ways that generate more than offsetting returns.

Public-private sector partnerships can also be used to advance certain international objectives. Particularly noteworthy are some recent health initiatives involving large foundations, national governments, and international organizations.[13]

Developing countries have demonstrated that they have the capacity to use efficiently substantially greater resources than they currently have access to. At one time, it was thought that global financial markets would make the provision of funding unnecessary for all but the poorest countries. We now realize that that is not the case. Funding goes to relatively few countries and relatively few sectors and is highly cyclical. The current crisis has highlighted the need for substantially more resources, especially in a time of crisis. Further exploration of innovative mechanisms for finance is clearly needed. Annual emissions of the Global Reserve Facility discussed in the first section of this chapter may be one possible source of substantial and stable funding.

6

CONCLUDING COMMENTS

This is the most significant global crisis in eighty years. The crisis is not just a once in a century accident, something that just happened to the economy, something that could not be anticipated, let alone avoided. We believe that, to the contrary, the crisis is man-made: it was the result of mistakes by the private sector and misguided and failed policies of the public.

WHAT WENT WRONG: A RECAP OF FAILED POLICIES AND PHILOSOPHIES

This Report is premised on the belief that if we are to respond adequately to the crisis—both if we are to have a robust recovery and if we are to prevent a recurrence—we must have an adequate diagnosis of the crisis. Both policies and economic theories played a role. Flawed policies helped create the crisis and helped accelerate the contagion of the crisis from the country of its origin around the world.

But underlying many of these mistakes, in both the public and private sectors, were the economic philosophies that have prevailed for the past quarter century (sometimes referred to as neoliberalism or market fundamentalism). These flawed theories distorted decisions in both the private and public sector, leading to the policies that contributed so much to the crisis and to the notion, for instance, that markets are self-correcting and that regulation is accordingly unnecessary. These theories also contributed to flawed policies on the part of Central Banks.

Flawed institutions and institutional arrangements at both the national and international level also contributed to the crisis. Deficiencies in international institutions, their governance, and the economic philosophies and models on which they relied contributed to their failure to prevent the crisis from erupting, to detect the problems which gave rise to the crisis and issue adequate early warning, and to deal adequately with the crisis once it could no longer be ignored. Indeed, some of the policies that they pushed played a role both in the creation of the crisis and its rapid spread around the world. All of this facilitated the export of toxic products, flawed regulatory philosophies, and deficient institutional practices from countries claiming to be exemplars for others to follow.

The debate about appropriate institutional practices and arrangements and the economic, political, and social theories on which they rest will continue for years. The ideas and ideologies underlying key aspects of what have variously been called neo-liberalism, market fundamentalism, or Washington Consensus doctrines have been found wanting. Other ideas, which might have been more helpful in avoiding the crisis and mitigating its extent, were overlooked.

The last quarter of a century has had some notable successes, not the least of which has been the rapid growth in Asia which has lifted hundreds of millions of people out of poverty and brought many benefits, including extended life spans, higher literacy, and improved health. But while some countries have done well, others have not. International financial and economic arrangements have in many cases worked to the disadvantage of developing countries. The global arrangements that have facilitated rapid growth in many parts of the world have not come without a cost: growing inequality in many countries and, in some cases, excessively rapid depletion of natural resources and degradation of the environment.

The last quarter century has also been marked by high levels of instability. In the past, the successes in preventing crises originating in developing countries from becoming global have come at a great cost, with many facing unnecessarily severe recessions and even depressions and with the assistance sometimes being accompanied by a loss of national sovereignty in matters of vital importance to a country's citizens. This, the Great Recession of 2008, is only the worst of the frequent crises that have plagued the world, but there was a complete failure in preventing this crisis that originated in the developed countries from bringing down with it even those developing countries that had put into place sound macro-economic and regulatory policies. While globalization offered the promise of greater economic stability, it has instead led to greater instability.

WHAT HAS BEEN DONE

The international community has responded to the crisis in an unprecedented way. The massive stimulus and rescue packages adopted by most governments have brought the world back from the precipice of a global depression. By and large, government expenditure policies to support economic activity have worked as predicted. In most countries these expenditures have been on productive investments so that new assets corresponding to the new liabilities have been created. Particularly commendable are the many stimulus packages that have included a "green" component, which addresses the major long-term environmental problems facing the planet at the same time that the spending enhances the strength of the global economy in the short run.

The substitution of the G-20 for the G-8 as the major forum for global discussions is to be welcomed, as it allows greater participation and includes some emerging markets. Yet the majority of the countries of the globe, whose voices need to be heard, are still excluded. There is particular concern about political legitimacy of discussion that excludes the voices of the least-developed countries. The Commission recognized the importance of combining effectiveness (which may be enhanced by the relatively small size of the deliberative group) with political legitimacy, and a key proposal presented has suggested how this might be done. It is essential for the success of any proposals for reform of the international trade and financial system that these concerns be addressed.

Also welcome are commitments to reform the international financial institutions. The agreement that the heads of the institutions would be chosen on the basis of merit is long overdue. Reforms in governance are essential if these institutions are to fulfill their mandates. Chapter 4 has provided an explanation of why the proposed reforms are not likely to go far enough and what additional reforms are desirable.

It now seems to have been recognized (even by those who pushed for deregulation) that there is a need for more, or at least better, regulation and enforcement, especially in the arenas of finance. But, as noted in Chapter 3, the task ahead is large, and it is not clear that there is yet an adequate understanding of the dimensions of the required action. The Commission, for instance, focused attention on the ways in which capital market and financial market liberalization and deregulation may have contributed not only to the creation of the crisis but also to its rapid spread around the world. Reforms must, moreover, go beyond finance, for instance, to laws and regulation affecting corporate governance, competition, and bankruptcy. Because the devil is often in the details, announcements of agreement on certain principles may not suffice.

While the numerous instances of protectionist actions which have been taken around the world, including by governments who had committed themselves to not doing so, have been a setback, matters might have been far worse without those commitments and an international framework designed to prevent such policies.

WHAT IS TO BE DONE

It is essential that, as the international community works for a robust and sustainable recovery and for reforms that ensure long-term, democratic, equitable, stable, and sustainable growth, it do so with a broader respect for a wide range of ideas and perspectives. At the very least, we need to be more modest about our confidence in particular economic theories, and our policies have to be robust enough not only to withstand shocks to the economy but also to hold us in good stead if some of the premises of our theories turn out to be wrong.

It is also imperative that policies be framed within a set of goals that are commensurate with a broad view of social justice and social solidarity, paying particular attention to the well-being of the developing countries and the limits imposed by the environment. It would be wrong and irresponsible to seek only quick fixes for this current crisis and ignore the very real problems facing the global economy and society, including the climate crisis, the energy crisis, the growth in inequality in most countries around the world, the persistence of poverty in many places, and the deficiencies in governance and accountability, especially within international organizations. To many, the crisis is but one symptom of a deeply dysfunctional set of global arrangements. Our Report approaches the current crisis from these broader perspectives.

We believe that a comprehensive agenda is required to attack the problems we have identified and to achieve the goals we should be seeking. This Report has focused on some of the Key Reforms in both national and international policies, regulations, and institutions. This is a macro-economic crisis, caused in part by micro-economic failures, bringing home the intertwining of these often disparate aspects of economic analysis and policy. Some analyses have focused on one, some on the other. We believe that these problems have to be approached from a coherent framework, and in this Report we have attempted to do just that.

SOME COMMON THEMES

There are several common themes that run through the analysis. One is that the growing inequalities in most countries around the world are not only socially unjust but have also contributed to the problem of potentially weak effective demand.

Another is that the crisis has to be seen as a *global* crisis. Accordingly, the responses have to be framed from a global perspective. The imbalances that marked the global economy in the years preceding the crisis were not sustainable; poorly designed responses, however, could exacerbate these imbalances. The high level of global volatility, combined with inadequate international arrangements enabling developing countries especially to manage this risk, has prompted many of the latter, at least those which had the means to follow an export-led strategy and to create their own self-insurance. This is one of several motivations which have led to the buildup of high levels of reserves, which also contributes to the global demand deficiency.

A third theme of the analysis is that there are large global asymmetries, illustrated by the differences in responses imposed on the

East Asian countries at the time of the last crisis and the policies pursued by developed countries in response to this crisis, which is a disadvantage of developing countries. These asymmetric responses may contribute to greater volatility in developing countries and thereby to a higher cost of capital, with adverse effects on growth and poverty. The problems are compounded by the fact that the poor countries have almost no say in the design of the rules of the game. Even allegedly symmetric rules, because they are applied in such a heterogeneous world, have strong asymmetric effects. Government guarantees to financial institutions by some of the advanced industrial countries contributed to the ironic situation of capital moving from the developing countries to those countries whose failed policies had caused the global conflagration.

A fourth is that the financial sector has systematically failed to perform its key roles of allocating capital and managing risk, all at low transactions costs. Governments, deluded by market fundamentalism, forgot the lessons of both economic theory and historical experience which note that if the financial sector is to perform its critical role, there must be adequate regulation.

A fifth is that economic globalization has outpaced the development of the political institutions required to manage it well. Economic integration implies increased economic interdependence, and that implies a greater need for global collective action, as illustrated by recent events. While this is a global crisis, policy responses are framed at the national level. The host of areas in which national governments have had to take action—from bankruptcy to competition policy to financial market regulation—now have to be addressed at the international level. Current institutional arrangements are not up to the task. They will either have to be reformed, or new institutions will have to be created. A strong, independent, and politically neutral body offering advice to relevant international institutions to improve their ability to shape economic policies in a sustainable and globally responsible way is necessary. In one way or the other, if our global economy is going to work for the benefit of the majority of the citizens of the world—and if it is to exhibit greater stability than it has in recent decades—something will have to be done. We cannot continue to let these problems fester.

A sixth and crucial theme, to which we have already referred, is the pervasiveness of externalities, one of several market failures that help explain why markets on their own are not necessarily either stable or efficient. These externalities are pervasive within countries and across borders. The failure of one financial institution contributed to weaknesses in others; the failure of the financial system to perform its core functions has imposed huge costs on society—on the economy, on taxpayers, on home owners, on workers, on retirees, on virtually everyone—and the world will be paying the bill for their mistakes for years to come. Mistakes in one country have imposed huge costs on other countries; in this case, the mistakes of a few developed countries have imposed large costs on many developing countries. Well-functioning globalization might have protected them; well-functioning financial markets might have shifted these risks from those less able to bear them to those who were more able. Neither globalization nor financial markets performed well.

The response to the crisis must recognize these externalities. Regulations in one country can have impacts on others. At a minimum there needs to be coordination of global financial regulation. While this crisis has become global, the responses to the crisis are designed at the national level, with a minimum of coordination between nations and with each country doing whatever it can to protect its own economy. The developing countries—including many that managed their monetary, fiscal, and regulatory powers far better than those in the advanced industrial countries from which the crisis emanated—have been put in a particularly disadvantageous position, as the problems of unfair competition, that they simply can't match the subsidies and guarantees of the wealthy countries, are compounded with a lack of resources to conduct countercyclical fiscal policies.

A seventh theme concerns *innovation*. Financial markets prided themselves on their innovativeness. Yet they failed to innovate in ways that led either to more sustained growth or greater stability, that enabled ordinary citizens to manage better the risks which they faced, and that enabled risks to be effectively shifted from those who are less able to bear them to those who are more able. Indeed, some of the innovations may have contributed to the problems: they enhanced problems of information asymmetries, and the increased complexities made assessments of risk harder and therefore the management of risk more difficult. Some of the innovations were directed at circumventing accounting and financial regulations that were designed to ensure the efficiency and stability of the financial system. The notion sometimes put forward that more regulation may stifle innovation may be false: better regulation may direct entrepreneurial talents to innovations that enhance societal well-being. We believe that modern technologies combined with advances in the understanding of economic processes have enhanced the scope for such innovations, and we have devoted considerable efforts at identifying some of the institutional innovations that might contribute to improvements in the well-being of ordinary citizens and to the functioning of the global economic system.

While discussions of the failures of markets have focused on the financial sector, it should be clear that some of the key problems are more pervasive. Flawed incentive structures that led to excessive risk taking and shortsighted behavior were, in part at least, a result of problems in corporate governance, which are manifest elsewhere. The problems of too-big-to-fail, too-big-to-be-resolved banks (discussed in Chapter 3) are a reflection of inadequate competition laws and/or deficiencies in enforcement.

A final theme is that in responding to the exigencies of the moment, we must take care not to worsen the underlying problems. This crisis should be seen as an opportunity to engage in necessary reforms. Historically, moments of crises often provide a rare chance for fundamental reforms that would otherwise be impossible. But there is also a danger: existing power structures can seize hold of these moments of crisis and use them for their own benefit, reinforcing inequalities and inequities. There may be a greater concentration of economic and political power after the crisis than before. This has happened in the past and seems to be happening in this crisis in certain countries, as the share of the too-big-to-fail banks has increased even further.

SOME KEY RECOMMENDATIONS

This crisis poses a deep question: can we have the benefits of globalization without bearing all of its most adverse costs? Can we manage the global economy in ways that enhance the well-being of most citizens around the world? We believe we can. We can at least manage the world economy much better than we have. This Report presents a large number of recommendations that suggest how this can be done, focusing, in particular, on how we can reduce the risk of the kind of crisis that the world has just experienced and how we can respond to the crisis in ways that especially help the poorest countries.

We have proposed short-term remedies—measures that can and should be taken up immediately—as well as longer-term actions, which may take months, even years, of debate. In some areas, such as the reform of financial regulations, we have provided rather specific recommendations (e.g., on the treatment of derivatives or the too-big-to-fail banks). In other cases, we have laid out a menu of options: we believe that a new global reserve system is absolutely essential, but there are many alternative designs, some of which would provide better macro-economic stability and some of which might enable the international community to address a number of other social and economic objectives. It should also be clear from what we have already said in these concluding remarks that we believe it is absolutely essential to create better institutional arrangements for coordinating global economic policy—for instance, along the lines of the Global Economic Coordination Council and International Panel of Experts discussed in Chapter 4.

The international community has recognized that it is both a matter of fairness and a matter of self-interest that something be done to help the developing countries. This Report has urged that more needs to be done. Too large of a fraction of the funds being provided are short-term loans; there is at least some risk that the effects of the crisis may be felt for a considerable period of time. It would not be in anyone's interest for there to be another debt crisis. We have emphasized that the funds that are provided must not be accompanied by the counterproductive pro-cyclical conditions that were often imposed in the past. While we have argued for a diversity of arrangements for the disbursement of funds and for critical reforms in existing institutional arrangements, we have also suggested that there is a need for a New Credit Facility, with a governance structure more in accord with the times and more responsive to both those providing the funds and the borrowers, thereby engendering greater confidence from both.

If this crisis has taught us nothing else, it has reminded us of the magnitudes of the risks confronting all economies, even those that are well managed. We need to admit that our systems of risk management, including the sharing and transferring of risk from those less able to bear them to those more able to do so, leave much to be desired. Our systems of resolving cross-border defaults, including restructuring sovereigns faced with the threat of default, are not what they should be to deal with 21st century globalization, nor are the institutional arrangements for handling cross-border commercial disputes or ensuring effective global competition. In some of these arenas, we have provided concrete suggestions on the way forward; in others, we have simply flagged the issue, hoping that others will follow up and develop alternative approaches.

The Commission has emphasized that, even after fixing the financial system, the problem of insufficiency of aggregate demand is likely to persist, making it imperative to begin work on some of the more fundamental reforms, such as in the global reserve system. These persistent problems also make the design of the "exit strategy" from existing stimulus policies of particular importance. Premature or unbalanced withdrawal of stimulus spending or government guarantees could impair a smooth recovery and exacerbate global imbalances.

The Commission drew its members from a diverse set of countries, backgrounds, and perspectives. The long hours of discussions and debates, extending over more than half a year, with meetings in New York, Geneva, Kuala Lumpur, Berlin, and The Hague, helped develop an understanding of the perspectives of each of the members and an appreciation of their viewpoints. This Report reflects the consensus among the members of the Commission that emerged out of these long deliberations.

In the course of our deliberations, we issued a Preliminary Report (in February 2009) and an Interim Report (in May 2009). We have been pleased with the reception that these reports received. We have incorporated many of the helpful comments and suggestions we have received.

As we note in Chapter 1, our Commission is but one of several efforts to address the challenges posed by this crisis. Readers of this Report will notice a considerable overlap between what we have said, and, say, the Communiqués of the G-20, but they should also note the important differences. Whether one agrees with the conclusions of the Commission, we believe that the issues that we have raised have not been adequately dealt with to date and cannot be ignored. Nationally and internationally, they must be addressed. These include, for instance, the deficiencies in the existing global reserve system and the development of too-big-to-fail and too-big-to-be-financially resolved financial institutions. Policies of financial and capital market liberalization need to be looked at from new perspectives. Bank secrecy not only is a problem for tax compliance but also poses a problem for developing countries fighting corruption, and the problems occur sometimes in major money centers and not just offshore. Most importantly, if we are to make globalization work, we will need to have better—more democratic, with a greater voice for developing countries—institutional arrangements for managing it.

This crisis is complex and multi-faceted, as have been the issues that we have attempted to address. We cannot hope, in a short Report like this, to resolve all the issues that are in dispute. Our ambition is more modest: to convince the international community that there is room for improvement—substantial scope for improving the efficiency and stability of the world economy, especially in ways that promote the well-being of all, especially the less-developed countries and the poorest people in all the countries. They have been among the innocent victims of this crisis.

If we are to live together in peace and security on this planet, there must be a modicum of social justice and solidarity among the citizens of the world. We must be able to work together to protect the world from the ravages of climate change, to help each other in times of global crisis such as that confronting the world today, and to promote economic growth and stability in the long run.

The UN is the one inclusive international organization with the political legitimacy and the broad mandate to address all of these issues and to take into account, in a comprehensive way, all the relevant dimensions of the policies designed to address these global economic, social, and environmental challenges. The UN and the various institutions that constitute the UN family were borne of previous crises—World War II and the Great Depression. This global crisis provides an occasion to strengthen the UN and its role in global economic governance. That is why the members of the Commission welcomed this initiative of the President of the General Assembly. The work of the Commission has reflected the broad concerns and mandates of the United Nations but with a particular focus on the impact of the crisis and of the policies designed to respond to the crisis and prevent a recurrence on the less-developed countries and emerging markets and on the poor in all countries.

This Report provides an outline of some of the reforms that we believe will help us move in the right direction. If it widens the space for more open debate on these issues of such vital importance to all of us, it will have fulfilled its missions, and all of our hard work will have been for good purpose.

NOTES

1. Congressional Oversight Panel, "Special Report on Regulatory Reform. Modernizing the American Financial Regulatory System: Recommendations for Improving Oversight, Protecting Consumers, and Ensuring Stability," Washington, D.C., January 2009, available at http://cop.senate.gov/reports/library/report-012909-cop.cfm.

2. In the United States, the regulatory segmentation introduced by the Glass-Steagall Banking Act of 1933 was progressively eroded from 1980 to 2000 and formally abandoned with the Gramm-Leach-Bliley (GLB) Financial Modernization Act of 1999. Under GLB, banks and other financial institutions were permitted to commingle banking, insurance, and securities activities within a holding company structure. At the time, the promoters of such legislation emphasized the benefits of diversification and ability to compete with foreign institutions that were permitted to combine these activities in one institution. Little concern was voiced about conflicts of interest among the various dimensions of the business, or about the commingling of risky activities with the core activities of the payment system and deposit protection. The Group of 30, under the leadership of Paul A. Volcker, in its January 2009 report *Financial Reform: A Framework for Financial Stability*, has called for establishing "new constraints on the type and scope of their risk-taking activities" for those institutions that carry the major responsibility for maintaining the financial infrastructure.

3. Rent-to-own provides household goods for a low weekly or monthly self-renewing lease payment without any down payment or credit check. The lease provides the option to purchase the goods. Payday loans are cash advances made at extremely high interest rates that are secured by the borrower's personal check to the lender, covered on the next payday with the borrower's next paycheck.

4. Major reports about the future of the WTO, such as the Sutherland and the Warwick report point into this direction and provide concrete proposals.

5. There may be other reasons, such as the need to provide for an aging population that would lead countries to adopt policies to increase domestic savings and hold them in the form of foreign assets. The associated "imbalances" would then simply reflect differences in the propensities of countries at different stages of development and with different age structures of the population to save and invest. Financial flows would then be from developed countries with high saving, aging populations to developing countries with younger populations and higher returns on investment. However, this has not been reflected in the statistics on international capital flows. Restrictions on the ability to use industrial policies to encourage nascent industries in emerging countries (as many of the currently industrialized countries did in earlier phases of their development) under recent WTO agreements may have led some countries to substitute exchange rate policies to effect similar outcomes, and this too may have contributed to reserve accumulation.

6. These reserves are sometimes called "owned reserves" to differentiate them from "borrowed reserves," whose counterparts are foreign capital inflows.

7. In the current system, SDRs are both booked as assets and liabilities on the central banks' balance sheets. This is reflected in an IMF account. Therefore, at the moment, SDRs are not considered as deposits in the IMF.

8. The Latin American Reserve Fund was created by Andean countries in 1978 and was then called the Andean Reserve Fund. Its current members are Bolivia, Colombia, Costa Rica, Ecuador, Peru, Uruguay, and Venezuela.

9. This initiative works as a system of bilateral swaps by member central banks, which are in the process of becoming multilateral. The system has not been used so far. ASEAN has a swap arrangement of its own that has a longer history.

10. As the conflicts over bankruptcy law in many countries demonstrates. The argument put forward by lenders that better (or more debtor-friendly) debt restructuring mechanisms might increase interest rates needs to be viewed with skepticism. It is obviously self-serving. We have suggested that all could benefit from better debt restructuring mechanisms. A more debtor-friendly system would induce more due diligence on the part of lenders. The current system, where the public sector has to repeatedly pick up the pieces as a result of deficient credit assessments by lenders, should be viewed as totally unacceptable. Debt crises impose large costs on society that go beyond the costs imposed on borrowers and lenders. Hence, even if lending rates increased, this may be beneficial.

11. See United Nations, "Doha Declaration on Financing for Development: outcome document of the Follow-up International Conference on Financing for Development to Review the Implementation of the Monterrey Consensus" (A/CONF.212/L.1/ Rev.1), Doha, Qatar, 29 November-2 December 2008, paragraph 67.

12. However, the introduction of these securities must overcome some practical difficulties. One possible set of concerns is associated with lags in the provision and frequent revisions of GDP data as well as over the quality of these estimates, but these issues should be easy to resolve through international standard setting and provision of technical assistance. More important in this regard is how to manage concerns that have been raised about the liquidity of such instruments, especially when they are newly issued. Such concerns were similarly raised when inflation indexed bonds were first introduced, but they are now accepted worldwide. Governments and multilaterals can help create a deeper market.

13. There has also been experimentation with new mechanisms for financing and incentivizing research. An example is the Advanced Market Commitments through which government donors commit funds to guarantee the prices of vaccines once they have been developed, provided they meet a number of criteria on effectiveness, cost, and availability. This helps encourage pharmaceutical firms to focus on research into neglected diseases which mainly affect poor countries. These mechanisms may, however, be inferior to other ways of funding and motivating research because they typically rely on the patent system, so that those who purchase the vaccine without assistance have to pay a price far in excess of the marginal cost. These problems are addressed by alternative financing/incentive schemes, such as prize funds.